CW00741343

The POLAR OCEAN CHALLENGE

The POLAR OCEAN CHALLENGE

The Story of a Teenager's Epic Voyage Around the North Pole

Ben Edwards

First published in Great Britain in 2018
Copyright © Ben Edwards and Simon Butler 2018
Design © Freelands Media Ltd 2018
Graphic artwork by Adrian Stone © 2018

British Library Cataloguing-in-Publication Data
A CIP record for this title is available from the British Library

ISBN 978 0 85704 328 3

HALSGROVE
Halsgrove House,
Ryelands Business Park,
Bagley Road, Wellington, Somerset TA21 9PZ
Tel: 01823 653777   Fax: 01823 216796
email: sales@halsgrove.com

Part of the Halsgrove group of companies
Information on all Halsgrove titles is available at: www.halsgrove.com

Also visit: http://polarocean.co.uk and https://wickedweatherwatch.org.uk

Printed and bound in India by Parksons Graphics Pvt Ltd

Contents

Northabout *approaching Volodarsky Island.*

Departure day (16 June 2016) for the Polar Ocean Challenge crew aboard Northabout *at Bristol docks. Ben's mother, Ros Edwards, says goodbye to her son at the quayside. Ros would be joining the crew in Tromsø and then on to Murmansk to start the second leg of the voyage through the North East Passage.*

Foreword

by Andy McNab CBE, DCM, MM

WHEN BEN WAS SIX YEARS OLD, I remember both of us sitting down at the kitchen table drawing monsters with crayons. As we drew, he explained to me with great excitement that one day he was going to fly on the back of a Pteranodon. I didn't know what a Pteranodon was at the time, so I just nodded and agreed that it sounded very exciting. Back then, I thought he was just a small boy with a vivid imagination. But clearly, I was wrong. Ben had already started a journey that may yet see him riding on the back of any dinosaur. Why not? He has the drive, the determination, and an enormous lust for life that can make just about anything happen.

But Ben is much more than this. He may not know it yet but he is also an inspiration, not only to his own generation but also to older generations who can so easily form negative views about our young people today.

What I hope this book demonstrates to all generations, is that it is never too early, or too late, to go out there and discover more of our planet and of ourselves. Once you start that kind of voyage of discovery, you never want to stop. Ask Ben, he'll tell you. He is still in training for that Pteranodon ride.

Ben speaking to camera for his video blog as Northabout *nears Point Barrow, Alaska.*

Preface

Sir David Hempleman-Adams KCVO, OBE, KStJ, DL, FRSGS

BEN EDWARDS WAS FOURTEEN when he embarked upon what many would consider to be their 'adventure of a lifetime'. Not he – for as the reader of this book will discover, Ben is not one to sit around for long and has already made a return trip to Greenland on board *Northabout* and, as described in the final chapter, he is preparing for further adventures in the near future both at sea and on land.

Ben with David at the helm aboard *North-about* sailing from Murmansk into the Barent's Sea at the start of the North East Passage.

The world is shrinking and the Golden Age of exploration and discovery, in which men (for it was then exclusively a male preserve) set off into the unknown, is now long past. Flight, satellite navigation and instant communication from even the most remote parts of the world ensure the almost impossibility of becoming lost. For those left at home it is possible to follow an expedition every step of the way via websites, blogs and TV news channels.

I was fortunate to sail with Ben and the crew of *Northabout* through both the North East and North West Passage routes on the Polar Ocean Challenge in 2016. As expedition leader I oversaw the fulfilment of my ambitions not only to complete the first circumnavigation of the North Pole in a single season, but in doing so to bring the world's attention the effects of the warming oceans and the rapid ice melt that has wrought such extraordinary and rapid change to our polar regions.

Ben played a vital role in the expedition's success. His presence aboard *Northabout* helped enormously in promoting my educational charity, Wicked Weather Watch – aimed at schools to help increase students' awareness of changes to our rapidly warming world. As it turned out, Ben was the only crew member to complete all four legs of the voyage and thus, through his daily blogs and video reports, he became the charity's ideal ambassador.

But equally satisfying was to be able to witness the change in Ben himself as he faced up to every challenge the expedition threw at him and which he describes with typical understatement in this book. He is not alone among his peers to look positively at the future but those of us who hand on an uncertain future to his generation should be thankful for their cheerful intelligence and determination to succeed.

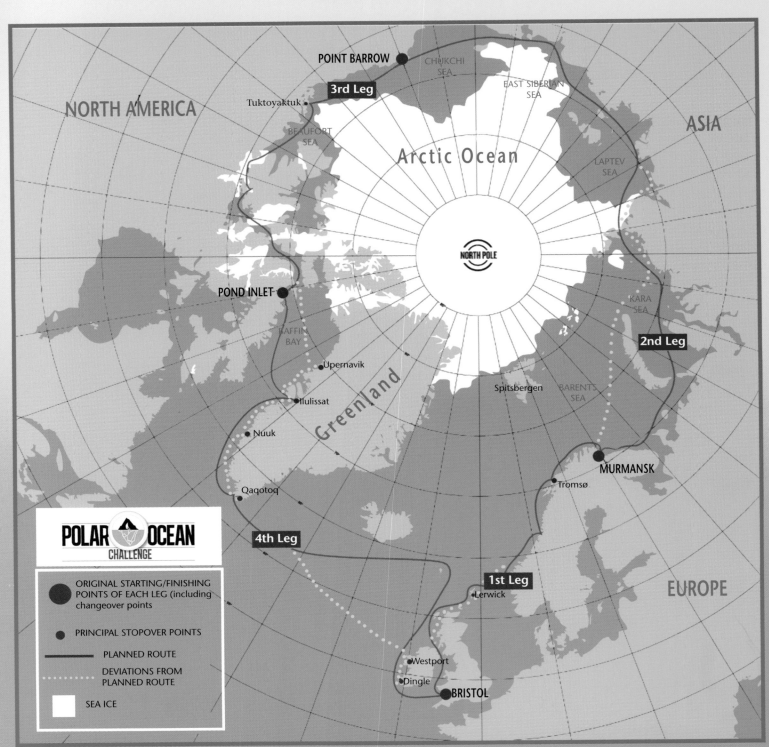

POINT BARROW

3rd Leg

Tuktoyaktuk

NORTH AMERICA

BEAUFORT
SEA

CHUKCHI
SEA

EAST SIBERIAN
SEA

ASIA

Arctic Ocean

LAPTEV
SEA

NORTH POLE

POND INLET

BAFFIN
BAY

Greenland

KARA
SEA

Upernavik

2nd Leg

Ilulissat

Spitsbergen

BARENTS
SEA

Nuuk

MURMANSK

Tromsø

Qaqotoq

4th Leg

1st Leg

Lerwick

EUROPE

POLAR OCEAN
CHALLENGE

Westport

Dingle

BRISTOL

ORIGINAL STARTING/FINISHING
POINTS OF EACH LEG (including
changeover points

PRINCIPAL STOPOVER POINTS

PLANNED ROUTE

DEVIATIONS FROM
PLANNED ROUTE

SEA ICE

Introduction

AS THE SAYING GOES even the best laid plans don't always go to plan and the original date of departure, in 2015, for the Polar Ocean Challenge had to be delayed for a year while *Northabout* was put in order. The old girl, by the time expedition leader David Hempleman-Adams found her, had already proved her Arctic credentials having been built in 2000 specifically to take on the North West Passage. Her builder, Jarlath Cunnane and his Irish crew, had then, in 2004, tackled the more demanding North East Passage before laying up the boat at her home port of Westport on the west coast of Ireland. But she had been laid up for some time and, as it turned out, was in need of some TLC before embarking once again for the polar oceans.

For David the delay was a frustration, and costly, for such expeditions are time-critical but he recognised that his first responsibility was to the safety of the crew and, as described later in this book, *Northabout*'s mechanical condition gave no guarantee that she would complete the circumnavigation – even discounting the perils of ice

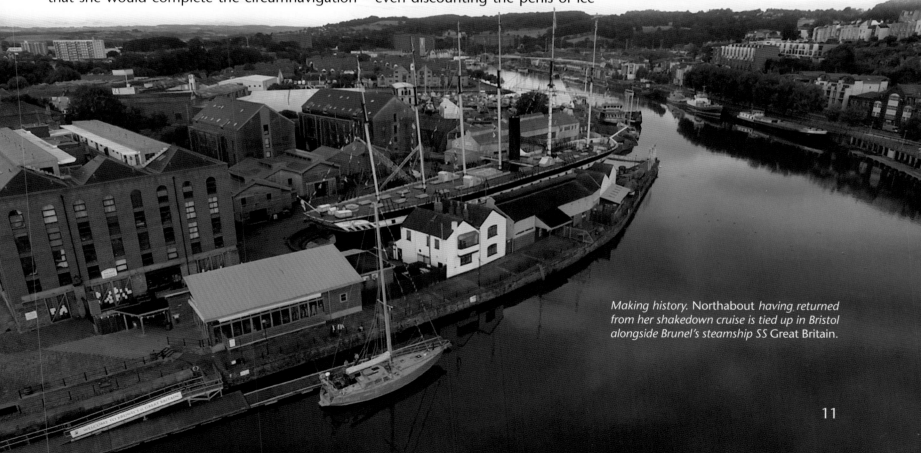

Making history. Northabout *having returned from her shakedown cruise is tied up in Bristol alongside Brunel's steamship SS* Great Britain.

11

and storm. It was thus decided that the main expedition would be delayed for a year while a comprehensive refurbishment of *Northabout* was undertaken, followed by a shakedown cruise to Svalbard (Spitsbergen) to uncover any further glitches. As it happened the Svalbard trip revealed enough problems to require several months' more work, partly under the eye of Ben's father, Steve, who by now had become fully committed to the expedition.

For Ben, his place on board *Northabout* came about in part as compensation for his missing out on an earlier expedition to the South Pole in which his mother, Ros, and an older sister had taken part under David's leadership. With sixteen being the cut-off age for participants imposed by the Antarctic support company, Ben had not been able to go despite David's complete confidence that he was more than able – and he consequently offered Ben a place on his next venture, the Polar Ocean Challenge.

David's mission statement for the Challenge defines his motivation:

I see this possibility to circumnavigate the Arctic as one I wanted to take despite the risks associated with it in order to increase the worlds attention on the effects of Arctic climate change. There may be a possibility still to curb this progressive warming and melting in the Arctic. But even if this is not possible the next most important thing is to at the very least highlight the need to 'Navigate the Future of the Arctic responsibly'. Shipping will pass through very soon, the lives of people living in the normally year round ice bound communities, well, their lives will change drastically. As are the habitats of walruses, whales, seals, polar bears, the whole ecosystems within the sea. We

Ben's father, Steve Edwards, who, after breaking his leg on the Svalbard trip, undertook the third leg of the Polar Ocean Challenge. Thus, literally, rather by accident than design he also became a lead figure in the fitting out of Northabout *after the shakedown cruise.*

Ben and Sir David Hempleman-Adams on watch aboard Northabout. *David, ever aware of his responsibility as expedition leader had only praise for his fourteen-year-old crewmate who 'started as a boy and returned a man'.*

can try to have an impact in trying to make sure that this change is handled carefully, sustainably, responsibly. I believe that all of us can be part of that conversation.

I have also set up a charity called Wicked Weather Watch which is an education based program engaging with schools on the issues of climate change, notably in the Arctic area. This is because it is the polar regions that I am most familiar with and where it would appear, certainly in the Arctic that climate change is very noticeable. Non scientist people like myself who, because I have been travelling to the polar regions for over 30 years now, have been witness to those changes first hand and bring another perspective alongside the scientific observations.

As for Ben, his original intention had been to take on the North East and North West Passages, the second and third legs of the Polar Ocean Challenge, with Ros and Steve undertaking perhaps one or two legs themselves. As it turned out, with Steve putting more effort into the fettling of *Northabout* and Ros undertaking the provisioning of the vessel for the voyage, their roles somewhat unexpectedly became more strategic, whilst Ben's role as a crew member expanded. Besides, as Ben himself declared, 'As the plans for the trip developed I felt more strongly that it would be important to me to complete the whole voyage, rather than to dip in and out. Personally I began to feel that to do otherwise would detract from the fundamental ethos of the Polar Ocean Challenge, for it to become simply adventure tourism.'

As this book describes, based entirely on conversations with Ben and his first hand accounts taken from the crew's logs, the voyage was by no means without danger and frustration and overcoming both the psychological and physical demands of the four months at sea ensured a test of character that, only on reflection, brings the most satisfying of rewards from any adventurous undertaking.

More than an adventure, the Polar Ocean Challenge was set up to bring to wider attention the dramatic changes in the Arctic and to highlight the need to 'navigate the future of the Arctic responsibly'.

David Hempleman-Adams had set up the Wicked Weather Watch charity in 2009 in order to provide a single source of information about global warming aimed specifically at children and schools. The Polar Ocean Challenge offered the perfect opportunity to link the two projects. Daily updates by the crew via blogs and video posted on the PoC and WWW websites provided followers with an vivid picture of conditions in the polar seas. Because of Ben's age, he was an ideal front man for communication with the youthful Wicked Weather Watch watchers.

Svalbard

The Shakedown Cruise and the refitting of Northabout

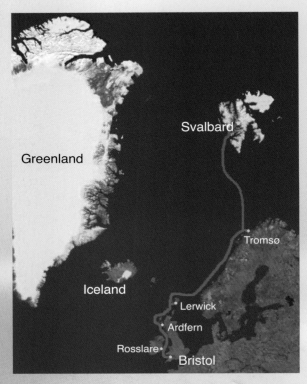

The track taken by Northabout *on her shakedown cruise in 2015 en route to Svalbard.*

ALTHOUGH POSING A MASSIVE HEADACHE for expedition leader David Hempleman-Adams, the decision to delay the Polar Ocean Challenge for a year was a blessing in disguise. *Northabout*, though soundly built and proven in Arctic waters, was well into her second decade and, to David's eye, needed refurbishment. As it turned out this proved to be a somewhat over-optimistic first impression for once the vessel arrived in Bristol early in 2015, his project managers made it clear that *Northabout* was far from ready to take on the Challenge. Reluctant as he was to delay departure – every month's delay meant rising costs and difficulties in retaining sponsors and keeping the crew together – David recognised that safety at sea came first:

In retrospect, the shakedown, which had first appeared to me as a huge disappointment and a headache in meeting ever-rising costs, turned out to be the platform from which the success of the Polar Ocean Challenge later sprang. I can say with some confidence that the later voyage, if not ending in failure, would certainly have been beset with problems that would have made the passage in a single season quite unlikely. From the tiniest niggles in the galley, to the major issues with the engine, we now had a chance to iron these out.

It would be also true to say that the Svalbard voyage itself uncovered rather more shortcomings in the vessel than had first been identified and, as detailed in the following pages, a great deal more work was required than first anticipated.

For Ben, whose mother and father also signed up, the Svalbard cruise provided an opportunity to get to know the vessel and also some of the crew members who would also be taking on the PoC. He would also be able to put into practice many of the things he learned on taking the RYA Competent Crew Course and, later, the Day Skipper Course at the East Anglian Sea School in Suffolk. Ironically, though passing the latter course he was, by two years, too young to receive the certificate!

While Ben and his family made up a third of the intended crew the decision as to who would skipper the boat was not decided until fairly late in the day. While David himself and Steve Edwards both had extensive ocean-going experience, David finally appointed Magnus Day as skipper, now in his late thirties, a sailor familiar with both Arctic and Antarctic waters. His second in command was the celebrated Russian sailor, Nikolai Litau whom David had already earmarked as skipper for the PoC and who would act as second mate on the outward voyage only of shakedown cruise.

Magnus Day, Skipper on the Shakedown cruise.

Nikolai was born in 1955 in North Kazakstan. After serving in the Soviet Army he attended university in Moscow and, aged 32, began life as a sailor eventually getting his skipper's ticket. From 1996 to 1999, as captain of the yacht *Apostol Andrey*, Nikolai successfully navigated the Northern Sea Route, becoming the first to sail round the world in the meridian direction for which exploit he was awarded the prestigious Medal for Seamanship. In 2002 he became the first to navigate the North East Passage on a yacht and subsequently took the *Apostol Andrey* on further circumnavigations of the globe.

Destination Svalbard. Northabout lies at anchor amid broken ice and awe-inspiring mountains.

In all Nikolai has surpassed 150 000 miles under sail and his presence on board inspired confidence among the less experienced crew although, certainly on the later voyage, the Russian proclivity for vodka and the seemingly endless supply on board caused raised eyebrows on more than one occasion.

Ben recalls his relationship with the taciturn Russian with grudging affection. 'He was just fine so long as one didn't do anything too stupid or ask too many silly questions. His capacity for drink was disconcerting but he certainly knew his way around a boat and navigated with supreme confidence.'

*　　　*　　　*

With a certain amount of hullabaloo, necessary to keep the sponsors happy, *Northabout* weighed anchor in Bristol docks on the morning of Sunday 2 August 2015 en route for Svalbard. Snaking her way down the River Severn with Brunel's bridge suspended high above the gorge the scene provided Ben and his six fellow crew members with a memorable start to their voyage – an occasion to be repeated a little under a year later on the PoC. High above circled the drone, its camera capturing the scene for later uploading to the Wicked Weather Watch website.

Clearing the Bristol Channel and heading north under sail towards the Irish Sea the forecast showed heavy weather ahead and Magnus reefed sail as *Northabout* entered the busy shipping lanes approaching St George's Channel. On day two, with winds predicted to increase to Gale Force 9, and with Ben, Steve, Constance and Barbara all seasick and thus leaving the watch shorthanded, it was decided to sit out the storm at Rosslare on the Irish coast. Here, Northabout tied up among the sheltering fishing boats waiting for the storm to clear.

Nikolai Litau.

DAVID HEMPLEMAN-ADAMS' BLOG
August 2015

Taking the bull by the horns, and aware of the fact that on his own navigations of both the North East and North West passages Nikolai had been obliged to overwinter, I ask him point blank on his thoughts of our chances of making it through in a single season.

"No way," was his immediate response. But after a vodka or two, he agreed that it might be possible, and that he would – for a fee – sign on as skipper for the Polar Ocean Challenge, with his colleague Denis Davydov as first mate.

Shortly before the start of the Svalbard voyage, crew members and those who were to join Northabout *in Svalbard pose aboard with the Mayor of Bristol, George Ferguson. From left: Ros Edwards, Mimi Edwards, Steve Edwards, David Hempleman-Adams, Barbara Fitzpatrick, George Ferguson, Constance Difede, Nikolai Litau, Magnus Day and Ben.*

Leaving Bristol, next stop Rosslare.

Our drone's view over the picturesque anchorage at Ardfern.

BEN'S BLOG
5 August 2015

We have now left Rosslare where we stayed when cowering from the scary wind. We've just reached the Mull of Kintyre in Scotland and hope to reach Ardfern by early tomorrow morning. The best thing of all about yesterday though was that I started using seasickness tablets and am still feeling fine. I also, after an unforgivably long time, realised why making tea on the onboard cooker is so tricky. It's not on gimbals, which usually keep the cooker the right way up if the boat is heeled over. For those of you who have a gruesome fascination with how difficult it is to go to the toilet in bad weather sailing gear on a floor that's at a 45 degree angle at two in the morning I must disappoint you. It's not that tricky. Making the tea is harder.

17

Learning the ropes. The shakedown cruise provided all the crew the chance of getting to know Northabout's *sailing qualities and for the more novice crewmembers the opportunity to learn from the experienced hands aboard. Here Magnus looks on as Ben handles the sheets on a rolling deck. It was around this time that the rig for the genoa sail started to give trouble requiring repairs in Ardfern.*

The following day, with the winds now perfect for sailing, the crew rigged the genoa and enjoyed the thrill of *Northabout* forging her way through the white-tipped waves like a real thoroughbred, covering 160 nautical miles in 24 hours. Only the quantity of commercial traffic in the relatively narrow seaway threatened *Northabout's* headlong progress during which Nikolai's skill at the helm came into its own.

Rapid though this progress was, the boat itself began to reveal a series of technical and mechanical problems which, though more or less alarming, at least confirmed the wisdom of delaying the PoC in favour of the shakedown cruise. While a note was made of any significant defects that needed to be fixed on return to Bristol, any immediate problems had to be dealt with while under sail. Again Nikolai, who trained as a mechanical engineer before he took to the sea, proved his value, and along with Steve's expertise in dealing with electronic glitches, *Northabout* reached her next port of call relatively intact.

For Ben, after five days at sea, their arrival at the pretty little port of Ardfern on the west coast of Scotland, meant stepping ashore for the welcome use of a shower and toilet that remained stationary, before tucking into a hearty breakfast. This brief stopover had been planned by David who, somewhat at Magnus's insistence, had arranged to pick up a massive sea anchor which, indeed, proved its worth later on.

Northabout *passing beneath the Skye Bridge after leaving Ardfern.*

The camera drone's view over Lerwick with Northabout tied up alongside the quay.

Lerwick schoolchildren visiting Northabout wave at the camera drone.

Then on to Lerwick in the Shetlands, two days' sail from Ardfern, where David had arranged a meeting with an old schoolfriend now teaching at the local primary school. Here was an ideal opportunity for Ben to record a video for the Wicked Weather Watch website and for the children to learn something about the aims of the PoC. Ben duly visited the school and the children had a chance to visit *Northabout* moored alongside the quay. These video diaries and the daily blogs compiled by Ben later became an integral part of the PoC, appearing regularly on the website.

Not long after leaving Lerwick the crew experienced the first major breakdown at sea. The engine, vital should the vessel be caught bad weather and important for manoeuvring in and out of port, stopped. Used to its steady beat the first signs of trouble came with intermittent coughs and splutters, occasional misfirings that initially righted themselves. But eventually the engine coughed and died leaving an eerie silence as *Northabout* slowly began to lose way. With Nikolai and Magnus investigating, the cause was identified as contaminated fuel blocking a filter – soon rectified, but another cautionary tale for future reference.

Fish and chips aboard Northabout in Lerwick on the eve of our departure for Tromsø. From left: Constance, Barbara, Ben, Magnus and David.

*   *   *

Sailing north found a noticeably prolonged daylight and when night did fall the horizon was punctuated by the flares of distant oil platforms, a reminder of how few parts of the globe are not under the hand of man. Three days after leaving Lerwick they crossed the Arctic Circle, always an occasion for celebration and not one to by missed by Nikolai who introduced the crew to the Russian custom of knocking back shots, one of vodka and one of seawater!

Ben and Magnus celebrating crossing the Arctic Circle on the way to Tromsø.

Below: Ellie and Ben on route to Svalbard.

After six days at sea and despite a persistent headwind *Northabout* heads up the channel into the harbour at Tromsø, passing almost unbelievably picturesque scenery of the Lofoten Islands on either hand. Here Eloise Daniel has flown in to join the crew, acting as cook, although a severe bout of sea sickness somewhat limits her in that role. Here for the first time it's decided that a washing-up rota is required on board.

On the 18 August *Northabout* is again at sea and the following day Bear Island hoves into view marking the approximate halfway point between Tromsø and Svalbard. As they approach the archipelago it becomes clear why the island group was first given its name, Spitsbergen, or 'jagged mountains' as translated from the Dutch. On the horizon the glacier-riven mountain peaks rise up, the scenery growing ever more magnificent as they sail onward.

On the morning of 22nd *Northabout* glides serenely into the harbour at Longyearbyen, Svalbard's largest settlement. Then disaster. If a reminder were ever needed among those who take up the challenge of adventure in testing environments, however much care is taken, bad things will occur. Taking a line in hand, Steve steps from the deck in order to tie up alongside. Losing his footing on the plastic edge of the pontoon it is immediately apparent that, in falling, his leg is broken. For his fellow crew members, and for Ben in particular, the episode is in that instant almost the worst imaginable.

For David the accident was certainly a test of his responsibility as leader of the expedition. A veteran of many testing adventures, including walking to both Poles, climbing Everest and solo ballooning across the Atlantic, his inbuilt reactions for dealing with emergencies were well honed. Finding the nearest medical centre closed, he demanded they get their act together and finally got the attention Steve urgently needed, an X-ray confirming two fractures to Steve's tibia. A flight was arranged back to the UK the following day where Steve could receive more extensive treatment.

Northabout *dwarfed by the 'jagged mountains' of Svalbard.*

Magnus and Nikolai examine all that remains of a seal having been taken on to a small ice floe and consumed by a polar bear.

David later confided that, following this incident, Nikolai (who initially had agreed to skipper *Northabout* on the forthcoming PoC) at this point expressed severe doubts as to the fitness of vessel and crew for such an undertaking. However, this accident aside, Nikolai later agreed that the shakedown cruise had been a success, that the crew had performed well and that, subject to further refitting, *Northabout* was more than capable of taking on the Arctic.

*   *   *

Northabout *dwarfed by a glacier.*

BEN'S BLOG
25 August 2015

Upon leaving Longyearbyen we noticed that there were a lot of seals in the fjord. I looked in the book on wildlife in Svalbard and I think that they were Harbour Seals. Actually, Svalbard's wildlife was a big part of the day yesterday. When we are anchored, if you go outside, you have to have a good look around to see if there are any polar bears. It's slightly unnerving, having to, when you leave your house, make sure that you aren't about to be attacked by a bear. Although we do have methods for repelling bear attacks, we have guns obviously. Although before I this trip started I was asked by a surprisingly large number of people, but you wouldn't actually shoot a polar bear would you? Unfortunately the answer to that question is: if it was running towards me then yes, I would shoot a bear. However, we don't just have guns, we have a hand held fog horn to scare it off and we have a wonderful thing called Bear Spray, brilliant! It's just really really strong pepper spray that you are supposed to use on Polar Bears. It's not very nice for the bear but it's better than shooting it.

Following Steve's accident and the planned departure of Nikolai, Northabout becomes home to a new set of crew members. From left: Ben, Rob Crout, Ros Edwards, Magnus, Mimi Edwards, Ellie Daniel, David Hempleman-Adams.

Northabout moored alongside a disused quay at the ghost town of Pyramiden, a former Russian settlement and coal-mining community on Svalbard. Closed in 1998 it has since remained largely abandoned with most of its infrastructure and buildings still in place.

With Steve safely back in the UK the crew, though thoroughly shaken, could at least look forward to taking in the wonders of the landscapes around them. Ben also had the arrival of his mother, Ros, and younger sister, Mimi, to look forward to. Indeed their arrival brightened the whole crew and gave added impetus to their exploration of the islands, their people and wildlife.

The last week of August 2015 saw *Northabout* at the end of her successful shake-down cruise and, if not in shape to immediately tackle the PoC, at least with David and her crew aware of what needed to be done during her refit.

Ben carrying his sister Mimi ashore having arrived in the RIB from Northabout, moored in the distance.

Back at the boatyard in Sharpness, under the eye of Colin Walker of Walker Planning and Construction, the shipwrights were given a short window from the start of April to mid June in which to complete a considerable list of repairs and upgrades. Steve Edwards, now with his broken leg rapidly mending, also took a greater interest in *Northabout*'s refit, particularly the installation of new electronics for control and navigation and the safety and emergency gear. Colin Walker takes up the story:

The starting point was to make sure the fuel system was clean and reliable so we removed all the old fuel, cleaned the tanks and installed a dual filter system, this means if one filter gets clogged we can easily switch over to the 2nd filter. We also needed to make sure there was enough fuel for the Eastern Passage so we checked the existing fuel capacity and found we had 5 tanks which gave 1700ltrs of fuel, we then added another 300ltr of emergency fuel in the stern locker. We needed to manage the fuel and control the flow from each tank so we installed a manifold and a Day Tank, this means we can easily isolate a tank if it gets contaminated when refuelling. The engine was given a full service and all the pipes replaced.

The boat has a lifting keel and the old system was very unreliable so Sharpness came up with a clever hydraulic lifting system that would hold the keel in place.

We needed to make sure there was sufficient power for the general day-to-day use of the boat plus for the electronics so we doubled the storage capacity of the domestic batteries and installed a small independent generator. This means we can generate

Steve Edwards took great care in selecting the navigation systems. Here Ben, his son, helms with the aid of the Raymarine display.

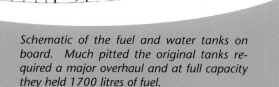

Schematic of the fuel and water tanks on board. Much pitted the original tanks required a major overhaul and at full capacity they held 1700 litres of fuel.

power from the alternator on the main engine or by the new generator or by the solar panels installed on the deck.

Installed a new water maker which has been loaned to Northabout for the trip.

Upgraded all the electronics on the boat to give reliable boat speed, wind direction and depth. Installed a new Raymarine solid state radar unit that can be used to spot icebergs. Installed 2 satellite communication systems so we can keep in touch with the outside world and more importantly gather the latest weather and ice data.

Upgraded the anchor winch as the anchor needed to be oversize to cope with the conditions Northabout is likely to experience. We had all the rigging checked and upgraded various winches etc....

We had the boat dry docked and Sharpness Boatyard replaced the propeller and shaft, we also repaired the rudder and anti fouled the boat. Re-wired the boat and checked the inverter so we could be sure we have a reliable 24 volt supply for the bread maker and microwave oven.

Maximised the storage area around the boat so we could store 3 months worth of food, including emergency provisions.

Installed a liferaft bracket on the transom and secured a 10 man liferaft. Purchased two 15HP 2 stroke outboards for the inflatable which could be used to help pull the boat off the ice if needed. We carried out a lot of carpentry work and added insulation.

Thus, with a huge amount of work and expenditure to match, by late spring 2016 *Northabout* was ready to take on the Polar Ocean Challenge.

The Perkins Sabre engine was fully serviced.

Much of the interior was refurbished.

Nearing completion late spring 2016. Note the new liferaft bracket and transom.

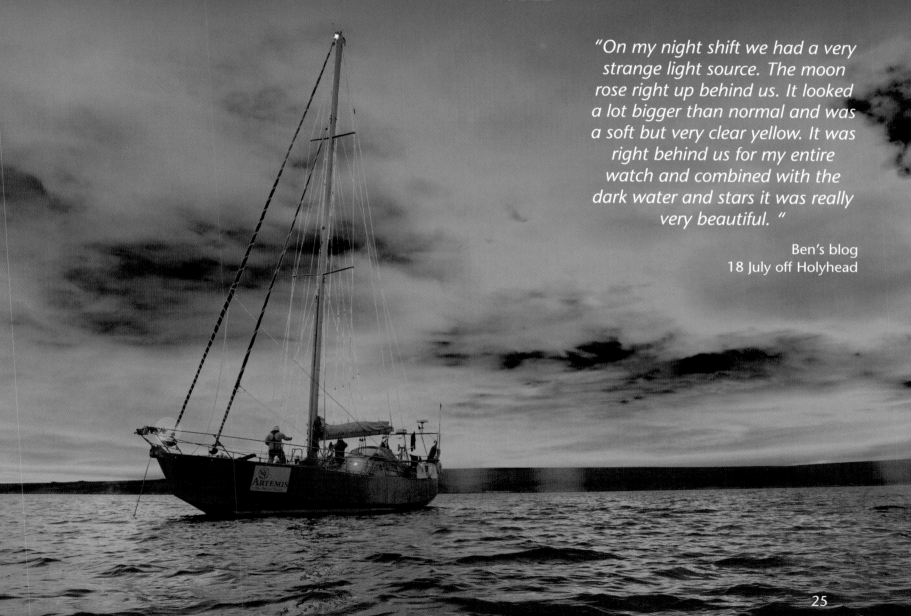

"A tall ship and a star to steer her by..."

NORTHABOUT – A SPECIAL KIND OF VESSEL

"On my night shift we had a very strange light source. The moon rose right up behind us. It looked a lot bigger than normal and was a soft but very clear yellow. It was right behind us for my entire watch and combined with the dark water and stars it was really very beautiful. "

Ben's blog
18 July off Holyhead

Utilising every inch of space on board.

The 'facilities'.

Ben, more than any other crew member, got to know *Northabout* the most intimately. Being the only person to complete the whole four month voyage, inevitably he experienced more hours aboard but also, perhaps because of his relatively novice ocean-going experience, *Northabout* became his alma mater of seamanship. Nor was she an easy mistress: the idiosyncracies of her behaviour both under sail and while motoring required a sure touch at the helm, while harmonious relations living at close quarters with his older crewmates demanded equal deftness on occasion.

Northabout had already proved her Arctic capabilities having already made, on separate voyages, both the North West and North East Passages. But she was now definitely past her carefree youth and entering middle age as sailing boats go – nearing her fifteenth year when David Hempleman Adams discovered her lying up in Westport on the west coast of Ireland. And the initial surveyor's report somewhat belied the owner's optimistic "Bejaysus! Turn the key and she's ready to go."

To be truthful, that individual, veteran sailor Jarlath Cunnane, knew *Northabout* better than anyone, for he had been responsible for her conception, that particular twinkle in his eye appearing as the last light faded on the twentieth century. In his superb book describing her adventures in the Arctic, titled *Northabout* (what else?), Jarlath takes up the story:

The boat we selected for our adventure was a Nadja 15 designed by Gilbert Caroff... one of three expedition boats he designed all of which made major polar voyages. In

Original blueprint of the Nadja 15.

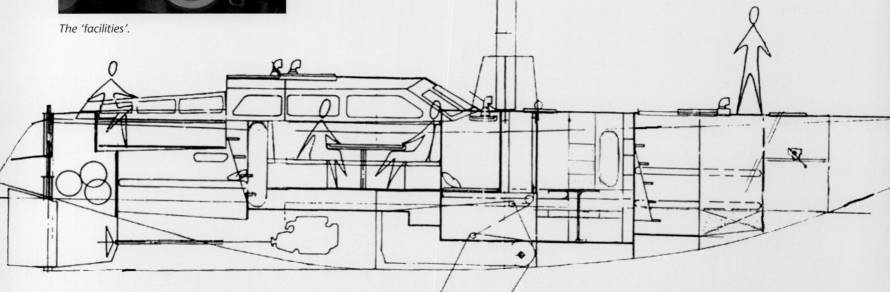

Strength in the original construction was essential if Northabout *was to withstand battering among the ice floes and the possibility of finding herself ice-bound. The use of aluminium in the hull, frame and stringers provided both strength and lightness. Here, in the year 2000, the hull is carefully lifted from the workshop ready for the fitting of the internal gear.*

Photo courtesy Jarlath Cunane

A 1909 replica of Henry Hudson's ship Halve Maen *in which he attempted to find a route through the North East Passage. This was his third Arctic voyage but, departing from Amsterdam in April 1609, he reached only as far as east of Norway's North Cape before finding his way blocked by ice. He then turned west, hoping to find open passage north of America but without success. He returned to Europe at the end of that year. The figures on board in the photograph give an idea of just how small the vessel was and how cramped the conditions on board for the crew of 20 men.*

Inset: Detail of Isaac Massas's map of 1612 based on Hudson's voyage and showing Samoyed figures, the 'wild men' of the Arctic region.

building Northabout *all components were selected as the best on offer for the task. For that reason a well engineered hull would be built. The mast, sails and rigging need to be stronger than normal. So much would depend on the reliability of the engine and machinery, and we gave our utmost attention to their selection and installation.*

For the earliest explorers in wooden-hulled vessels there was little knowledge to draw on regarding the perils of sailing the polar oceans. Would-be discoverers of the fabled North East and North West Passages, were drawn from all major maritime nations of Europe desirous of being the first to open up the routes that would bring wealth and fame to them and their nations, but the waters they entered held unknown dangers.

Among the first were the Dutch who, between 1594-1596, sponsored three expeditions under William Barentz to seek the North East Passage. On the third voyage, beset by ice, he and his crew were stranded on Novaya Zemlya for almost a year, Barentz himself meeting his death. Along with adventures such as sighting their first polar bear, which they captured and brought aboard with the intention of taking it back to Holland (they shot it when it escaped), they also battled walruses and met Siberian 'wild men'. But nothing prepared them for the relentless cold and implacable ice of the Arctic winter. They were among the first to record, in 1596, the terrors of a ship caught in the ice:

The 27 of August the ice drove round about the ship, and yet it was good weather; at which time we went on land, and being there it began to blow south-east with a reasonable gale, and then the ice came with great force before the bow, and drove the ship up four foot high before, and behind it seemed as if the keel lay on the ground, so that it seemed that the ship would be overthrown in the place; whereupon they that were in the ship put out the boat, therewith to save their lives, and withall put out a flag to make a signe to us to come on board: which we perceiving, and beholding the ship to be lifted up in that sort, made all the haste we could to get on board, thinking that the ship was burst in pieces...

Barentz's men attempt to capture a polar bear.

William Barentz's ship caught in the ice with the pressure lifting the bow high into the air.

It was experiencing the power of the ice once a vessel was gripped in its clutches that gave later mariners cause for greatest concern when venturing into polar seas. Vessels that had been designed for sailing in warmer seas were no match for the ever-moving mass of Arctic ice for which there were no navigational charts providing the way ahead, or the passage back home.

Even today, and notwithstanding claims and counter-claims about the effects of global warming, the extent and movement of sea ice is wholly unpredictable and, certainly, for those early mariners, sailing into northern waters was akin to setting forth to discover a new planet. However, for early nineteenth century adventurers, reports of the disappearance of Arctic ice between the years 1815-17, gave added impetus to their pioneering Empire-building spirit, added to which, at the end of the Napoleonic Wars, 'the Admiralty found itself in possession of large numbers of enterprising officers and thousands of unrequired ships'.

Of those thousands of surplus vessels a few were uniquely suited to Arctic waters: these were known as bomb ships, specialised vessels equipped with heavy mortars rather than canon. To withstand the shock from the recoil of these massive weapons the hulls of these ships were extremely strong and thus ideal for sailing in northern waters were entrapment by ice was a constant hazard.

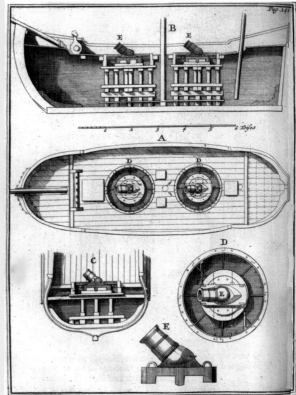

Bomb vessel plans showing the reinforcement of the hull required to support the massive mortars. A plate from Memoires d'Artillerie by Pierre Surirey de Saint Remy, 1745.

HMS Hecla and HMS Fury were bomb vessels converted for Arctic exploration work in the early 1820s and both took part in William Parry's various expeditions in search of a western passage between 1819 and 1825. On his second voyage, in 1821-23 Hecla was held fast in the ice at Winter Harbor on Canada's Melville Island for nine months. In 1825 HMS Fury was so badly damaged by ice during overwintering that she was abandoned at what is now Fury Beach on Somerset Island.

The drama of Arctic exploration became a favourite subject for marine artists of the day. Here William Smyth captures the perilous position of HMS Terror trapped in the ice during Captain George Back's 1836–37 attempt to discover a route through the North West Passage. The expedition's goal was the northern end of Hudson Bay from where they would drag boats overland to open water and sail the unknown coast west to the Back River and Franklin's Point Turnagain. A converted bomb vessel, HMS Terror, left England in June 1836 with a crew of 60 and provisions for 18 months but the lateness found Terror beset by ice somewhere east of Frozen Strait where she remained icebound for 10 months. At one point the vessel was pushed 40 feet up the side of a cliff by the pressure of the ice.

In the Royal Navy these ships were named after volcanoes and the most famous of these were HMS *Terror* and HMS *Erebus*, the former taking part in three major Arctic expeditions: George Back's expedition of 1836–1837, the Ross expedition of 1839 to 1843, and Sir John Franklin's ill-fated attempt to force the Northwest Passage in 1845, during which she was lost with all hands along with HMS *Erebus*.

A cutaway drawing of HMS Erebus, a former bomb ship specially converted for Arctic and Antarctic exploration. Her most celebrated voyage, along with HMS Terror, was under the command of Sir John Franklin in 1845 tasked with completing the first navigation of the North West Passage. The ships were last seen entering Baffin Bay in 1845 and the tale of their tragic end has remained one of the great stories of maritime history. Thirty-two metres in length, Erebus was fitted with a steam locomotive engine and a boiler that heated parts of the ship's accommodation and also supplied desalinated water for the crew. A further innovation was the tinned food the expedition took on board.

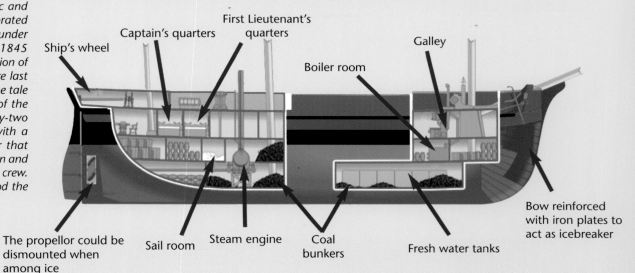

First Lieutenant's quarters

Captain's quarters

Galley

Ship's wheel

Boiler room

The propellor could be dismounted when among ice

Sail room

Steam engine

Coal bunkers

Fresh water tanks

Bow reinforced with iron plates to act as icebreaker

And it is not only the Arctic vessel's hull that needs to withstand the ice and extreme temperatures, as Jarlath Cunnane was aware whilst constructing *Northabout*, the mast, sails and rigging also needed additional strength. While in command of HMS *Dorothea* and HMS *Trent* on his polar voyage in 1818 Ross' ships met with a severe storm:

The snow fell in heavy showers, and several tons weight of ice accumulated about the sides of the brig (the Trent*) and formed a complete casing to the planks, which received an additional layer at each plunge of the vessel. So great indeed, was the accumulation about the bows, that we were obliged to cut it away repeatedly with axes to relieve the bow-sprit from the enormous weight that was attached to it; and the ropes were so thickly covered with ice, that it was necessary to beat them with large sticks to keep them in a state of readiness for any evolution that might be rendered necessary, either by the appearance of ice to leeward, or by a change of wind.*

At one point Ben and his companions aboard *Northabout* had to break ice away from the anchor cable where its accumulated weight threatened to submerge the vessel's bow.

*   *   *

BEN'S BLOG

July 2016
Anchored in the Nordenshel'da Archipelago just at the start of the Vilkitsky strait in the South Kara Sea

Yesterday was, I thought, very nice. It was about ten degrees outside, a very pleasant temperature for us at the moment. We had light winds and no fog. Things only kicked up a bit in the evening when the wind changed. The day before the wind had gone to the south and all the ice in the bay rushed past us and went up the northern end. When the wind changed to the west, it did the whole thing in reverse. And that is how Denis ended up standing on the foredeck at midnight with a large pole fending off bits of ice that threatened to hit the anchor chain.

Northabout *Skipper, Nikolai, and first mate, Denis, poling ice away from the hull. These ice poles are an essential bit of kit when sailing in Arctic waters and were used on a number of occasions during the Polar Ocean Challenge.*

No story better reminds those who would venture into the polar oceans of the perils of Arctic exploration than the tale of John Franklin's fateful expedition. The disappearance of his two ships HMS *Terror* and HMS *Erebus* in 1845 set in train a series of follow-up expeditions each intent upon solving the mystery, many simply fuelling speculation in what had happened to Franklin and the 129 men who sailed with him.

The first concrete evidence appeared when Hudson's Bay Company doctor John Rae collected artifacts and testimony from local Inuit in 1853. These people also told stories of sick and emaciated men hauling boats across the ice before eventually succumbing to scurvy and starvation. Speculation that they had resorted to cannibalism or had died as a result of poisoning through the tinned food on board was compounded as later expeditions came upon artefacts and skeletal remains. Then, in 2014, Canadian marine archaeologists discovered the wreck of *Erebus* and two years later that of HMS *Terror* lying in relatively shallow waters in Queen Maud Gulf. As the sunken vessels, both remarkably intact, are further explored so it will throw new light on this 150 year mystery.

*   *   *

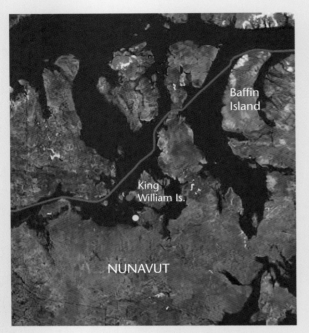

The final resting places of HMS Terror *(red dot) and HMS* Erebus *(yellow dot) close to King William Island. The red track is the route taken by* Northabout *through the North West Passage in 2016 on the third leg of the Polar Ocean Challenge.*

Among the purpose-built vessels built for Arctic conditions one of the most famed is the Norwegian explorer Fridtjof Nansen's *Fram*. Between 1893 and 1912 this groundbreaking vessel undertook two expeditions to the Arctic and one, having undergone an extensive refit, to the Antarctic under the command of Nansen's fellow countryman Roald Amundsen. Abandoned in South America at the outbreak of the First World War, *Fram,* now almost a wreck, was towed back to Oslo in 1935 where work began on her restoration. She now stands as a centrepiece in the Fram Museum.

Nansen's Fram *was a truly revolutionary design – a vessel that could withstand the crushing pressures of pack ice for several years should it be necessary. Constructed largely of oak and iron, the hull was immensely strong with naturally formed oak ribs laid only 5cm apart and clad in a sheath of greenheart that could be torn off by the action of the ice without seriously damaging the hull. Designed as a three-masted schooner* Fram *was powered by a steam engine and had electric lighting on board.*

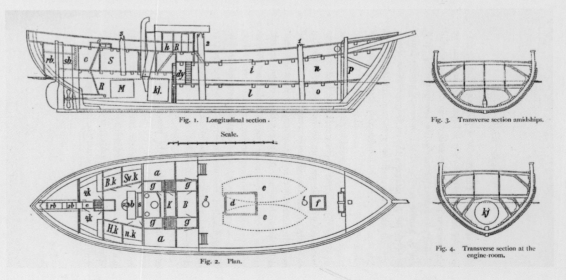

Fig. 1. Longitudinal section.

Scale.

Fig. 3. Transverse section amidships.

Fig. 2. Plan.

Fig. 4. Transverse section at the engine-room.

Bristol to Murmansk

The First Leg of the Polar Ocean Challenge

BY MID JUNE 2016 *Northabout* was almost ready to take on the Polar Ocean Challenge although there was still work to be done completing the refit which meant Steve travelling from Bristol to Tromsø to oversee the configuring of navigation and communications systems and consequent sea trials.

For Ben, now committed to take on all four legs of the circumnavigation, the planned four-month voyage, assuming the ice allowed free passage, would mean a significant time out of school. Asked if his school engaged in the impending voyage on its own website Ben reflects with typical coolness: 'They were generous in allowing time off school and concerned that I should not do anything that reflected badly on myself or on them, but as far as my schoolfriends were concerned they knew I was leaving school early to do something that involved a boat sailing to a cold place, but otherwise they showed little interest.' This was certainly not true of the press and TV media who gave a great deal of space to interviewing Ben both before and during the voyage. During these interviews Ben was able to outline his duties on board *Northabout* and also his expectations of the conditions and dangers likely to be faced. He was also able to emphasise the more serious purpose of the expedition in bringing to wider attention the effects of global warming.

In the course of a number of TV interviews the media naturally focused on Ben's relative youthfulness in taking on the Polar Ocean Challenge. Here at Whiteness on Shetland, wearing his PoC T-shirt, Ben is explaining to a TV crew his thoughts and motivations: 'I want to be the first British person to sail around the North Pole in a single season, and also the youngest person. But also it's simply likely to be an amazing experience and I hope to be able to see it through to the end.'

BBC NEWS 20:51 NS: bbc.co.uk/terms HEADLINES BARACK OBAMA ENDO

Ben interviewed live on BBC News shortly before the expedition gets underway. Asked why he wanted to take on the journey, Ben responds, 'Well, partly because last year my older sister walked to the South Pole and I want to go one better!' More seriously he explains to the presenter his role as ambassador for Wicked Weather Watch and the part he will play in promoting the voyage, via his blog, through the Polar Ocean Challenge website.

Addenbrooke's Charitable Trust

Another interview, another T-Shirt. As a sufferer from a mild form of IBD Ben chose to raise money for the work of Addenbrooke's in supporting fellow sufferers. Though diet plays a part in controlling the disease, Ben himself ate the same food as everyone else on board Northabout – except by his own admission many more chocolate biscuits than some.

BEN'S BLOG

16 June 2016
Sharpness

For first leg of the trip (Bristol to Murmansk – Russia y'know. The big country that's always in spy films). David isn't here and Magnus isn't on the trip at all. Instead, our skipper is a man named Dave Cushing; my Dad's on board until Tromsø too. The rest of the crew for that leg are: me, Annie, John, Clive, Colin and Hazel. All the usual suspects join us later, Nikolai, Barbara, David and so on. We leave on Sunday and it's half 11, we've a four-thirty start tomorrow so I should probably go to bed, I'll write again tomorrow, and whoever is posting this, last year, Mum cut off the last paragraph before posting, please don't do that.

Ben also had a personal commitment to raise money for Addenbrooke's hospital in Cambridge to aid research into Inflammatory Bowel Disease in children. Suffering himself from a mild form of IBD he hoped by completing the voyage he would encourage others not to become victim to their illness. 'I see this trip partly as proving that so long as you're pig-headed enough, there's very little that can stop you.' In truth there was some parental concern regarding his condition, as Ben recalled: 'Everyone in the family accepted there was some risk in going on the trip, something stress related perhaps, and we carried on board some very strong pain killers and antibiotics in case of a serious problem. Apart from these preparations if anything major was to happen then I accepted that things would either turn out fine, or that it would be too late to get to proper medical help.'

*　　　*　　　*

With 16 June 2016 being set as the departure date from Sharpness, the weeks beforehand saw frantic activity aboard *Northabout*; loading provisions and last minute checks of equipment. David Hempleman-Adams had finally persuaded Nikolai, for a fee, that he should be skipper for the whole of North East and North West Passage legs of the trip, a responsibility Nikolai accepted on condition that his compatriot, Denis Davydov, was taken on as first mate. Their presence, along with David's contacts in Moscow, helped overcome the tortuous process of securing permits for sailing in Russian waters. Along with these two veteran Russian sailors David had also secured on board a large quantity of Mamont vodka!

Ben on board with members of the Thornbury Sailing Club, leaving Sharpness.

David himself, however, having recently been appointed High Sheriff of Wiltshire, had to forego his presence on the first leg of the PoC. With Nikolai not joining *Northabout* until Lerwick, and Denis joining her in Murmansk, this left the vessel severely shorthanded for the first leg. The day was saved by Steve Beacham, owner of the dry dock at Sharpness, who suggested that members of nearby Thornbury Sailing Club would jump at the chance of crewing Northabout as far as Lerwick.

Major General the Revd David Coulter, Chaplain General, holds a service of blessing on board Northabout *before departure.*

The first leg crew and those who will join Northabout *later wave goodbye to friends, family and well wishers at the dockside.*

35

On a dull morning, with farewells said to friends and family at the quayside, *Northabout* once again glides through the deep gorge beneath the Clifton suspension bridge and out through the widening channel of the Severn estuary, scene of many mishaps due to racing tides and shifting mudbanks, but skipper Dave Cushing expertly navigates their way to the open sea. As if to celebrate the start of the voyage a pod of Dolphins appears and the crew are entertained as they play alongside.

As often the case, the first hours at sea can affect even the most seasoned sailors before the peculiarities of the vessel's motion mixed with the faint smell of diesel and salt air become familiar. For those being sick and those not there is an uneasy truce based on equal measures of sympathy and schadenfreude. Ben's blog of 19 June perfectly illustrates the scene on board:

Anyway, we left the Bristol Channel and everyone was fine. I was on watch first and it was all absolutely fine. Almost everyone was on deck for the first few hours. They all enjoyed the sunshine and the beautiful sea, until Milford Haven. At that point some of us started to feel ill. I was off duty so I went off to bed. Dad doesn't have a watch, he's our resident techie so he's exempt. He went off to bed until midnight. Hazel got it worst. I was feeling fine by ten o'clock, which is when my shift starts, so I went up on deck and did my bit. At twelve, Dad came up feeling much restored and kept me and Annie company. At two o'clock Hazel came up looking completely terrible. Tired and on the verge of throwing up, she came on deck, and vomited into a bucket. I got up at half eight and had a bacon roll.

But as they approach St George's Channel, the serenity aboard is shortlived and Steve's decision to sail on this leg is amply vindicated. Because of the tight schedule allowed for the refit, his suspicions that problems would occur were well founded when a routine check in the bilges revealed an ominously growing pool of water. Grabbing a torch the Skipper and Steve Edwards open the hatch above the still-revolving prop shaft and, there in the beam's light, they see a steady flow of water being thrown out

BEN'S BLOG
19 June 2016
Bristol

When I got off watch it was discovered that we had two or three inches of water in the bottom of the boat which shouldn't be there. Dad and Dave tried to fix this but, as it turned out, our bilge pumps are broken, yay. It was decided that we would head to Wales and get some guys from Sharpness up to fix it for us. So we headed east and we've docked in the Holyhead marina.

By the light of a torch, the crew discover the cause of the rapid water ingress in the bilges.

Dolphins in the Irish Sea.

BEN'S BLOG

20 June 2016 – Holyhead

While we were in Holyhead I restarted the tradition of buying a stuffed toy animal in every port we dock at and attaching it to the pulpit. In Bristol this year I got rat, and in Holyhead I got a sheepdog.

Ben's mascots. By the end of the PoC Ben's collection of good luck trophies formed a strange and somewhat soggy figurehead on North-about's pulpit.

from the stern gland bearing. With the pumps apparently unable to cope with the inflow a decision is quickly made to make for Holyhead on the Welsh coast.

Following somewhat frantic late night calls to David Hempleman-Adams, a party from the Sharpness boatyard drove up to Holyhead and quickly discovered the problem. The stern gland has a seal around the propellor shaft to prevent seawater leaking past the bearing and into the boat during normal operation, but here – exacerbated by the pumps being incorrectly assembled – was the cause of the problem. However, a few hours feverish activity and *Northabout* was once again on her way.

But troubles at sea seldom come singly and as *Northabout* and crew made their way north a catalogue of minor and not so minor niggles revealed themselves. An incorrect connection to the reverse osmosis water maker resulted in John Whitely taking an unwanted shower. The oven refused to work properly (and was later condemned by a gas engineer in Lerwick) and further teething problems cropped up with both the engine and the electronics. Some of these were of course to be expected after such a comprehensive refit and it was just as well they came while still in the benign waters off the British coast. It was also fortunate to have the experienced Thornbury people on board who were quick to spot potential problems that could be fixed before the expedition entered more hostile waters.

After a brief overnight anchorage in Ornsay Bay off the Isle of Skye, ten days after setting out from Bristol, on 28 June *Northabout* entered the sheltered habour at

BEN'S BLOG

20 June 2016 – Holyhead

It turned out that there was a problem with the reverse osmosis water maker. We had turned it on to see how long it took to get drinking water out of it, and half an hour later John was woken up by a cold shower. We later learned the feed of seawater to the water maker was not connected and the holding tank was filling up with salt water.

FIRST LEG
Bristol – Murmansk

POLAR OCEAN
CHALLENGE

Leaving Bristol on 19 June, Northabout arrived in Lerwick on the 28th. The first leg, from Bristol to Murmansk involved various crew changes, only Ben completing the whole leg, with Steve having departed in Tromsø. Nikolai Litau joined as skipper in Lerwick, while Ros Edwards flew up to Tromsø and joined there, with Denis Davydov and David Hempleman-Adams meeting the boat in Murmansk. The crew from Lerwick to Tromsø comprised Nikolai, Dave Cushing, Steve and Ben Edwards, Annie Green, John Harvey and Hazel Richards. Vardo was reached on 11 July and Murmansk on the 14th.

Lerwick. For the Thornbury crew this was the end of the line and John Whitely summed up what many of them were thinking: 'As the Shetlands come into view a small wave of sadness washes over me in realisation that this short sojourn is closing.'

Nikolai arrived, minus his laptop containing all his navigational charts which he'd left at the airport in Inverness (later retrieved), and immediately began the task of sorting out the necessary permits for entering Russian waters. For Steve and Dave Cushing arrival meant getting to grips with sorting out the repairs needed, including complete replacement of the stern gland seal (which had continued to leak), before setting off for Tromsø and then Murmansk on 2 July.

For Ben, as with the rest of the crew, arrival in port meant the luxury of finding hot showers and food that didn't have the tang of saltwater. It was also a chance to restock the on-board larders from the local Tesco.

Denied the use of the faulty onboard oven John Harvey's role as chief cook (left) kept the crew's spirits up on the first leg, but any chance to eat ashore was taken up with relish. Here Hazel, Annie, John and Ben make the most of breakfast at Perries Café in Lerwick.

Along with his general duties as crew member, Ben also found himself being volunteered for other tasks:

'When we got back from shopping it was announced to me that my father and David had been in touch with ITN and that I would be visiting a local school tomorrow with one of their cameraman. They've taken a special interest in us which is great, the more publicity we get, the more coverage Wicked Weather Watch and ACT get, Whoo! I'm going to be writing the occasional blog directly to them so I'm afraid if you want to read it you'll have to go on to the ITN website.'

Taking his ambassadorial role seriously, Ben tells the pupils of Whiteness School, Lerwick, about the aims of the PoC and the Wicked Weather Watch charity. The children also had a chance to dress in Ben's ocean sailing gear. Filmed by an ITN crew the occasion brought nation-wide publicity.

A final interview before departing Lerwick aboard Northabout *with the ITN news crew.*

Repairs completed, food stocks replenished and with a new skipper on board, *Northabout* sails out of Lerwick late morning on 2 July under sunny skies. From here the real voyage begins, sailing into the Arctic Circle and, as many explorers had done before, sailing into an Arctic ocean in which the ice may or may not allow free passage. A voyage which might, as the crew of *Northabout* hoped, be successfully completed in a single year, but which, as those early adventurers in these waters found, could see them imprisoned in the encroaching ice.

THE EXPLORERS

"Man cannot discover new oceans unless he has the courage to lose sight of the shore."
André Gide

Previous page: *Dramatic painting of HMS Assistance trapped in the ice, a painting by Thomas Robins (1810–1880). Built of teak in 1835 as a merchantman Assistance was later purchased by the Navy and, in 1850, took part in Horatio Austin's unsuccessful attempt to find Sir John Franklin's lost expedition. Retained for future Arctic service, the vessel sailed with Edward Belcher's expedition in 1852, became trapped in the ice off Bathurst Island, and was abandoned shortly after the scene depicted here.*

The polar regions have always had a huge attraction for mankind and its explorers. What lay in or beyond those icy wastes? An open sea? The way to Asia? Riches beyond the dreams of avarice? Many set out to find out, never to return. Probably no other field of exploration has brought forth so many heroes, sung and unsung, so much suffering and so many, often unnecessary, deaths. Probably most of the gruesome deaths in the icy reaches will never be known or told, but several did make it into print from the 16th to the 20th century.

What follows is a brief record of a handful of such expeditions, the only criterion being that they portray the hardships of Arctic exploration at their most extreme.

Sir Hugh Willoughby

A Derbyshireman (died 1554) Willoughby was an early English Arctic voyager. He was sent out in 1553, as captain of the *Bona Esperanza* with two other vessels under his command, by a group of London merchants known as the Company of Merchant Adventurers to New Lands, which later became the Muscovy Company. The vessels were separated by 'terrible whirlwinds' in the Norwegian Sea. On 14 September 1553 Willoughby sailed into a bay near the present border between Finland and Russia. The ships with the frozen crews, including Captain Willoughby and his journal, were found by Russian fishermen a year later. It has been suggested that Sir Hugh Willoughby and his crew were killed by carbon monoxide poisoning, following their decision to insulate their ship from the bitter Arctic cold. A 19th century woodcut shows him and his crew sitting dispiritedly on deck. The ill-fated voyage is harrowingly described in the book *Hakluyt's Principal Navigations*.

The end of Sir Hugh Willoughby, his ship trapped in the ice in a location thought possibly to be near Vardo.

William Barentz

William Barentz or Barents was a Dutch navigator, cartographer, explorer, and the leader of several early expeditions to the far north. The Barents Sea, Barentsburg and the Barents Regions were named after him. His career as an explorer was spent searching for the North East Passage which he reasoned must exist as clear, open water north of Siberia since the sun shone 24 hours a day, which he believed would have melted any potential ice.

The lodge built by dismantling Barentz's icebound ship in which he and his crew overwintered in 1596.

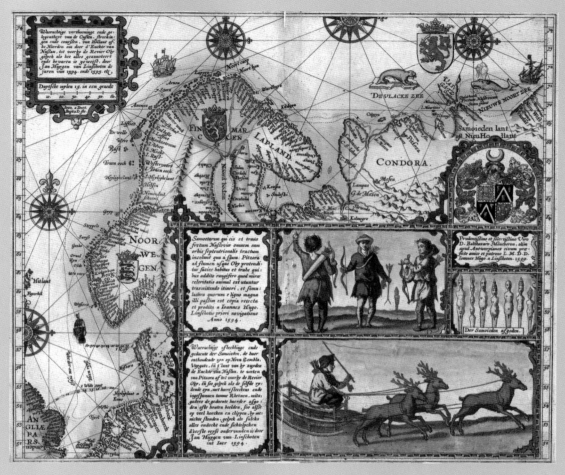

A map of William Barentz's first voyage in 1594, in which he set out to attempt to discover the North East Passage. In July the crew came across a polar bear for the first time which they attempted to capture to take back home. But the bear escaped causing havoc on board ship and had to be shot. Barentz reached the coast of Novaya Zemlya before being forced to turn back in the face of encroaching ice.

His first two expeditions, having set out with great hopes, both returned due to unfavourable ice conditions. In 1596 he set out again, hoping to win the high reward offered to anyone who successfully navigated the North East Passage. Barentz's ship was trapped in the ice near Novaya Zemlya close to where *Northabout* passed at the end of July 2016. Barentz and his 16-man crew was forced to spend the winter on the ice, dismantling their ship to build a lodge. They soon realized that their socks would burn before their feet got warmed by fire and took to heating stones and cannon balls to warm their beds, nearly suffocating when someone had the bright idea of keeping the warmth in the house by blocking the chimney. When the ice did not melt next summer, the crew, now ridden by scurvy, and with a very sick captain, built two small boats, and dragged them to the open water. Barentz died of malnutrition after seven days in one of the boats. Eventually, only 12 crewmen were rescued by a Russian merchant vessel and eventually found their way home again.

Henry Hudson

Hudson was an English navigator in the early 17th century. He made several voyages for the Dutch East India Company, searching for a shortcut to India, either around Russia via the North East Passage, or through a strait believed to be in Northern America, the North West Passage. He started on his final voyage in 1610 in his ship *Discovery* and, rounding Greenland, believed he had finally found the North West Passage. However, as they entered what is now Hudson Bay they were trapped by ice, and had to winter there.

When the ice cleared in the spring Hudson planned to continue his explorations, but the crew mutinied setting Hudson, his teenage son John, and six crewmen loyal to Hudson, adrift from the *Discovery* in a small open boat, effectively marooning them in Hudson Bay. They were never heard of again. John Collier's painting depicts the melancholy scene, with the father sitting in the stern of the boat, his son at his feet.

Upon their return to England, the crew placed the blame for the mutiny on two seamen, who had conveniently died during the return trip and the surviving eight seamen were acquitted of the charge of murder.

'The Last Voyage of Henry Hudson' by John Collier (1850–1934) imagines the melancholy last hours of the navigator and his crew.

John Franklin

Franklin's story epitomises the bravery and the folly of those early explorers who looked to conquer the North West Passage. Although greatly experienced in Arctic travel, at 59 years of age he was by the standards of his time, an old man. In 1845 he sailed the ships *Erebus* and *Terror* into the Canadian Arctic and became trapped in ice off King William Island, he and his crew never to be seen alive again. According to a note found on that island, Franklin died there in 11 June 1847.

After two years and no word from the expedition, Lady Franklin urged the Admirality to send a search party, the first of many. A reward of £20,000 was offered for finding the expedition. Eventually, more men and ships were lost looking for Franklin than in the expedition itself. The Scottish explorer John Rae discovered from Inuits that Franklin's ships became ice-bound, the men had tried to reach safety on foot but had succumbed to cold – though many refused to believe Rae. Then, in 1997, more than 140 years after Dr Rae's report, his account was finally vindicated; blade cut marks on the bones of some of the crew found on King William Island strongly suggested that conditions had become so dire that some crew members resorted to cannibalism.

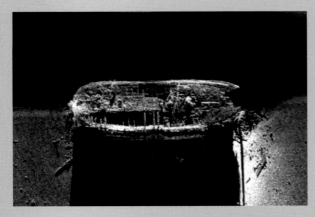

A sonar image of the recently rediscovered Erebus *found along with HMS* Terror *lying in relatively shallow waters in Queen Maud Gulf.*

Salomon August Andrée

The second half of the 19th century has been called the Heroic Age of polar exploration. The inhospitable and dangerous Arctic regions appealed to the imagination in the early age of flight, not as lands with their own ecologies and cultures, but as challenges to be conquered by technological ingenuity and manly daring.

The Swede Salomon August Andrée shared these enthusiasms, and proposed a plan for letting the wind propel a hydrogen balloon, the *Eagle*, from Svalbard across the Arctic Sea to the Bering Strait, to fetch up in Alaska, Canada, or Russia, and passing near or even right over the North Pole on the way. Modern writers all agree that Andrée's North Pole scheme was unrealistic. He relied on the winds blowing more or less in the direction he wanted to go, on being able to fine-tune his direction with the drag ropes, on the balloon being sealed tight enough to stay airborne for 30 days, and on no ice or snow sticking to the balloon to weigh it down. An attempt in 1896 found the wind blowing steadily from the north, straight at the balloon hangar at Danes Island, forcing the abandonment of the expedition.

Returning to Danes Island in the summer of 1897, Andrée and his companions, Nils Strindberg and Knut Fraenkel, found that the balloon hangar built the year before had weathered the winter storms well. The winds were more favourable, too. However, optimism overcame reality once again and Andrée ignored warnings concerning lack of steering, too little ballast and leakage of hydrogen through the balloon's canopy.

Salomon Andrée and (below) the route taken during his ill-fated balloon flight.

On 11 July 1897 the three explorers climbed into the already heavy basket and, as the large support team cut away the last ropes the *Eagle* rose slowly in the air. Immediately the long drag ropes, intended to help with steering the balloon, began to pull it towards the water and the crew were forced to jettison ballast in order to gain height.

Free flight lasted for 10 hours and 29 minutes and was followed by another 41 hours of bumpy ride with frequent ground contact before the inevitable final crash. The *Eagle* travelled for 2 days and 3½ hours altogether, during which time, according to Andrée, none of the three men got any sleep. The *Eagle* had been stocked with safety equipment such as guns, snowshoes, sleds, skis, a tent, a small boat fitted with skis into which the men, after a week camped next to the balloon, piled essential gear and set out across the ice.

What happened after this comes from diaries and photographs found intact many years later at the final resting place of the three men whose bodies were discovered in 1930 lying close to the skeleton of the boat, frozen in the ice.

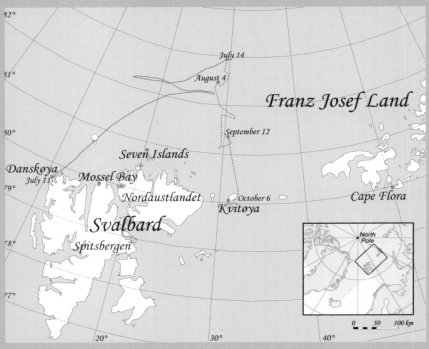

THE TRAILING ROPES FORCE THE EAGLE EARTHWARDS...

CRASH!

HAULING OVER THE ICE.

...A LONELY DEATH.

As Northabout ploughs steady north-north-east, towards Tromsø, her next port of call, the physical demands of sailing in open waters are becoming apparent through Ben's daily blogs while the occasional moment of celebration provides a welcome lift to the crew's spirits, as does the sighting of land:

I managed to sleep last night but come my first watch I kept on falling asleep and then suddenly waking up again. I'm not really surprised though. Before last night I'd slept two hours out of forty in the end. At three o'clock we passed the Arctic Circle. We turned the engine off and put the sails up for that. There was almost no wind so it took us half an hour to close the last hundred meters to the circle. While we were waiting I noticed something strange off the starboard bow, I could see land! After four days at sea I could see the characteristic jaggedness of Norway's coastline. It was only an island rather than the mainland but it was still exciting.

But even at night there are the occasional distractions to enliven the 'late shift' watches:

I got up ten minutes before my first shift, ten minutes later it started raining. This continued right to an hour before I went off shift when it cleared up. Now, six and a half hours later, it's raining again, worse than before. My shift was very boring. The night before, just after I finished writing, we went past an oil field. Oil rigs are divided into two types generally, the ones everyone thinks of, with the flame on the top and so on. I can't remember their names but they are more or less unmanned, people are flown out to them from what is called the Nodal Rig. Nodal Rigs are manned, they are where everyone eats, sleeps, stores things, land the helicopters for refuelling and so on. The Nodals are much larger than the others and have white rather than orange lights. I find that both types of rig are very pretty, at night at least.

Difficulties faced in watch-keeping – just staying awake.

Brightly lit rigs punctuate the night sky en route to Norway. Nodal rigs have crewmen aboard, while well-head rigs or NUIs (Normally Unmanned Installations) do not.

Champagne moment. The GoPro camera captures the time of crossing the Arctic Circle. From l-r: Ben, Annie (helming), Hazel, Nikolai, John and Steve.

BEN'S BLOG
5 July 2016

When sailing across the Arctic Circle there is a tradition. You are supposed to all have a glass of Arctic seawater, and then take the taste away with vodka. Hazel had brought champagne instead so it wasn't quite right. I had the sea water but then one of those small cans of coke for obvious reasons. I did a little piece on camera for ITN and then we planned to put a message in the champagne bottle, seal it, and throw overboard. We couldn't reseal the bottle so we poured a bottle of gin away and used that instead.

Two days after first sighting the Norway coast *Northabout* sails serenely through the spectacular inlets that lead into the busy port of Tromsø. Here Ros has flown in with daughter, Bea, and Ben and Steve take the opportunity to spend a couple of nights with their newly arrived family members in a hotel, catching up on sleep. A week before arriving in Tromsø, Ros adds her own blog to the PoC website which throws an interesting light on what went on behind the scenes:

Ros Edwards.

It is a week before I join Northabout *in Tromso. I'm sitting on a train on the way into London for a meeting, just arriving at King's Cross. It's 7.35am. The boat is in Lerwick getting some much needed TLC, the crew on the first leg having contended with a leaking stern gland and broken bilge pumps – casualties of the enormous amount of work that has been done on the boat in the last few weeks. I guess they are all up and working, possibly with the exception of our teenager Ben. The last few weeks have been hectic for our family. Steve, who is on the first leg and will re-join for the North West Passage, has been specifying the navigation and communications equipment and helping to conclude the re-fit; Ben, who is doing the whole circumnavigation from Bristol to Bristol, has had school and has been collecting all his homework for the trip; we have had one daughter doing A levels.*

I am so excited! Sitting in London imagining the water and ice and isolation – a reality dislocation. When I'm on the boat I won't give a second thought to my priorities for today – they just won't seem that important.

Ben, John and Steve preparing to tie up alongside the quay in Tromsø.

BEN'S BLOG
7 July 2016

I stayed in the hotel last night. Dinner was nice but I was tired so I left early and went to bed. I had been assured that I would be woken up at eight o'clock to have breakfast in the hotel, but the family decided that they would leave me to sleep in. Because of this I eventually woke up at half twelve local time. I went down to the boat and then immediately went out again for lunch. Then Mother and I went to the retail park that's near the airport because there were a few things we needed that we still didn't have.

David Hempleman-Adams, whose own dietary necessities for exploration ran to pork scratchings was more than relieved to have Ros, with her science background, take over the provisioning of the boat in readiness for the most arduous legs of the voyage. Now Ros insisted on the installation of a microwave with a built-in convection oven, and also two breadmakers. While these made additional calls on *Northabout*'s electrical systems the upgrading of this, in turn, ensured that overall the circuitry would stand up to the rigours of the PoC.

Steve discovers Tromsø's impressive library.

Dave and Nikolai preparing Northabout for the onward voyage to Murmansk.

49

Leaving the crowded marina in Tromsø on the morning of 9 July. From left: Hazel, Dave, Ben, Annie and Nikolai.

BEN'S BLOG
9 July 2016

At about nine we left the Tromsø and went to the fuel pontoon. As it turned out, John had the card that would allow us to get fuel. John isn't with us now because we were expecting a group of parts to turn up so that we could fix the generator. They weren't there. As a result John volunteered to stay behind and collect the parts before then catching a flight to Vardo, which is where Hazel is getting off. Just as we were leaving the fuel pontoon the steering jammed. We could turn to port but the rudder and wheel refused to turn to starboard. Because of this we had to return to the Tromso harbour. We got in, unpacked the aft locker and Nikolai went down to see what was wrong. What he found was a large piece of unidentified metal lodged in the drive shaft. Yeah, that would do it. So we repacked the locker and went back to the fuel pontoon. This time we took John so we could get some fuel. We finally left in the middle of my first watch and were sailing up the fjords again, Vardo bound.

With Steve leaving the boat, *Northabout* lost her resident 'techie' expert on the navigational and communications equipment but he had been able to help, with Nikolai, oversee the many general maintenance issues that were listed in the long 'Tromsø To Do List'. These included fitting the generator cooling system, fitting an engine bilge pump, removing the old oven and replacing it with the microwave, replacing a navigation running light and checking filters and engine oil.

Back at sea again. Ben on watch.

SEAL MEAT, SCURVY and SNICKERS

"I was somewhat taken aback to discover that even in the most remote places, there was always an opportunity to stock up on fresh food. Certainly in Murmansk, with its reputation for austerity and industrial grittiness, my illusions were somewhat shattered by discovering the supermarkets looked pretty much like those at home, clean, bright with shelves stocked with just about everything one could need – at cheaper prices."

David Hempleman-Adams

Seasoned leader of the PoC expedition David Hempleman Adams, with all the instinct for survival based on taking the minimum amount of equipment and food on his previous journeys, found the provisioning of *Northabout* somewhat perplexing but he was the first to acknowledge that modern expeditions, particularly those involving less seasoned explorers than himself needed to take proper precautions regarding the quantity and type of food to be taken.

Now, while I was more than happy to leave the victualling side of the voyage to an expert, I did draw the line at suggestions that we take a cappuccino maker (I'd also banned the idea of a DVD player) and raised an eyebrow when I saw several varieties of tea bag arriving on board: fruit teas, camomile, earl grey and so on, luxuries that cut against the explorer grain. Yet I had to admit that your favourite cup of tea arriving after a day of stress gives a wonderful lift to flagging spirits. One thing not accounted

Ros retrieving Mars Bars, Snickers and wine from the on-board lockers.

Stocking up on food in Murmansk where the supermarkets were provisioned as well as any at home, and at cheaper prices too.

for was the Russian predilection for vodka and dried fish of which Nikolai and Denis appeared to have a never-ending supply. While we were never short, I was always conscious of the need to conserve food in case we should be ice-bound at any time.

Bearing in mind that, at the outset, there was no guarantee of completing the circumnavigation in a single season, this could mean days or even weeks stuck in the ice waiting to be picked up, a period prolonged if the weather was against rescue.

David also found it interesting to witness the work of a professional scientist (Ros) in detailing what provisions should be taken, and why. And all parties were surprised to find well-stocked supermarkets in most of the places they stopped at en route, even in some of the most remote parts of the Arctic.

* * *

For the indigenous peoples of the Arctic regions hunting and fishing was their only reliable way of obtaining food and Inuit people were expert at this. Just as early explorers such as Nansen shunned any notion of adopting western clothing for his expeditions, preferring with good reason to wear what the locals wore, so seasoned explorers began also to rely on the Inuit for providing food.

In 1878-80, at the behest of the American Geographical Society, Frederick Gustavus Schwatka led an expedition to the Canadian Arctic to look for written records thought to have been left on or near King William Island by members of Franklin's lost expedition. The group, assisted by an Inuit, went north from Hudson Bay 'with three sledges drawn by over forty dogs, relatively few provisions, but a large quantity of arms and ammunition'. Though the expedition failed to find the hoped-for papers the party not only made the longest sledge journey ever made both in regard to time and distance of eleven months and four days and 2709 miles, it was also the first Arctic expedition which relied entirely on the same diet as the Inuit.

Writing just before leaving to join *Northabout* and its crew in Tromsø, Ros Edwards lists some of the food she will be taking with her:

I have been collecting a ton of food, literally, to provision Northabout for the North East and North West Passages: 16kg of hot chocolate, 20kg of Parmesan, and around 100 packets of biscuits – you have to get your priorities right. With a ton of food sitting in the hall visitors have been asking if we're expecting the apocalypse (or maybe just Brexit!).

Ros's words have resonances in Sir Francis M'Clintock's book *The Voyage of the Fox in Arctic Seas* published in 1859, the year after the Fox returned from its three-year voyage. M'Clintock was yet another explorer determined to discover Franklin's fate, and while unsuccessful, he was certainly determined not to fail through starvation:

Ample provisions for twenty-eight months were embarked, including preserved vegetables, lemon-juice, and pickles, for daily consumption, and preserved meats for every third day: also as much of Messrs. Allsopp's stoutest ale as we could find room for. The Government, although declining to send out an expedition, yet now contributed

BEN'S BLOG
July 2016 – off the coast of Norway

It's nice feeling fine. Nikolai has reorganised parts of the forward part of the boat so that you can now find things. This is also nice: for lunch I was introduced to the Glaswegian square-sausage. It tastes like toast!

Tempting? Ros on board *Northabout*.

Sir Francis M'Clintock
On eating seal meat

We had fried liver and steaks for breakfast this morning; both were good but the steaks were preferred; they were very dark and tender, had been cut thin, deprived of all fat, and washed in two or three waters to get rid of the blubber.

liberally to our supplies. The Admiralty caused 6682 lbs. of pemmican to be prepared for our use. Not less than 85,000 lbs. of this invaluable food have been prepared since 1845 at the Royal Clarence Victualling Yard, Gosport, for the use of the arctic expeditions. It is composed of prime beef cut into thin slices and dried over a wood fire; then pounded up and mixed with about an equal weight of melted beef fat. The warm pemmican is then run into strong tin cases and becomes hard on cooling; our cases contained 42 lbs. each, they were oblong in shape, but with convex ends, this form giving them greater strength to resist the claws of the Bears.

A soup tin, relic of Franklin's expedition retrieved from the ice many years later.

Since M'Clintock's voyage there have been more than ninety search parties determined on discovering what happened to Franklin. The use of tinned food, a relatively recent innovation in the 1850s was recently posited as having played a part in condemning Franklin's crews aboard *Terror* and *Erebus* to a slow death. In 1984, the bodies of three of the crew, John Torrington, John Hartnell and William Braine that had been found buried in the Canadian permafrost were exhumed. An autopsy found high levels of lead in the remains said to be enough to produce severe behavioural and physiological symptoms, even death.

While others have questioned the conclusions drawn, the fate of many early explorers was determined by their diet and access to fresh food from which to obtain Vitamin C, without which sailors succumbed to scurvy resulting in joint pain, rotting gums, leaky blood vessels, physical and mental degeneration. Such a fate befell yet another party sent in search of Franklin, setting out in 1853 under an American, Dr Elisha Kane on the vessel *Advance*. Twice overwintering in the sea between Ellesmere Island and Greenland, Kane is 'seized by a sudden pain' and faints, his limbs becoming rigid and his mind delirious. One by one his men fall victim to scurvy, symptoms including painful joints, loose teeth, swollen, bleeding gums, and bleeding both under the skin and in the bowels. Only after abandoning their vessel and making for the Greenland coast and reaching Upernavik are they saved.

The preserved body of John Torrington, a stoker on Franklin's expedition. An autopsy revealed high levels of lead concentration in his body.

With scurvy a bane of Arctic travellers, an enduring mystery was how did the indigenous peoples of the Arctic avoid a similar fate when their diet was almost entirely absent of fresh vegetables and fruit. The explorer Vilhjalmur Stefansson adopted an Eskimo-style diet for five years during the two Arctic expeditions he led between 1908 and 1918, declaring 'The thing to do is to find your antiscorbutics where you are,' he wrote. 'Pick them up as you go.' In 1928, to convince sceptics, he and a young colleague spent a year on an Americanized version of the diet under medical supervision at Bellevue Hospital in New York City. The pair ate steaks, chops, organ meats like brain and liver, poultry, fish, and fat with gusto. 'If you have some fresh meat in your diet every day and don't overcook it,' Stefansson declared triumphantly, 'there will be enough Vitamin C from that source alone to prevent scurvy.'

It's since been established that all it takes to ward off scurvy is a daily dose of 10 milligrams of vitamin C, easily supplied in the Inuit diet of organ meats especially when eaten raw. Samples of foods eaten by Inuit women living in the Canadian Arctic found caribou liver supplied almost 24 milligrams, seal brain close to 15 milligrams, and raw kelp more than 28 milligrams. Still higher levels were found in whale skin and blubber.

While polar bear meat is highly prized by the Inuit they avoid eating the liver which has proved fatal to early explorers succumbing to hypervitaminosis, an excess of vitamin, causing hair loss, extreme peeling of the skin, liver problems, vomiting, and blurred vision.

Natives of Siorapaluk, Greenland, butcher a narwhal watched by an eager crowd. Photographed on a 2017 visit to the island aboard Northabout.

DAVID HEMPLEMAN-ADAMS' BLOG
August 2016

Well before the expedition got underway, Ros had contacted all those intending to sail asking them to alert her to any dietary preferences or food allergies that would need to be considered. While few responded, Ros carefully made out a list of essentials from which a varied menu of meals could be prepared, taking into account Northabout's relatively primitive galley facilities, the mixed culinary skills of the crew, and the watches aboard which made meal times very much a movable feast. This meant that main meals followed a pattern during our passage through the polar oceans, each day a particular meal, with the pattern rotating over a week or more in order to provide variety while ensuring nutritional balance. A healthy quantity of non-essentials, biscuits and other snacks, topped up empty stomachs as and when required. And I swear, Ben could have eaten several pizzas and a couple of kilos of oranges at one sitting if he'd been allowed.

As for alcohol on board *Northabout*, while most of the crew looked with some amazement on the Russians' habitual use of vodka, it was also with some alarm considering the ever-present dangers and need for clear heads.

For Ros, her main objective in provisioning *Northabout* was to supply nutritious food convenient to store aboard a small vessel and not subject to spoiling. Against some resistance she also provided ample supplies of comfort food, appreciating that the prevention of occasional bad moods and low morale can simply be mitigated by the appearance of a chocolate biscuit or a cup of tea.

In this Ros shared the view of the early Arctic explorer William Scoresby who is mentioned in a report on Arctic travel written in the early 1800s setting out a regime for maintaining health and wellbeing:

Throughout the winter, the officers every day took a walk of two or three hours; but they never proceeded farther than a mile, lest they should be overtaken by a snowdrift. Exercise was also enforced upon the men, who, when prevented by the weather from leaving the vessel, were made to keep time while they ran round the deck to the music of an organ. Altogether, the health of the crew and officers was excellent. Special caution was exercised with regard to scurvy – an alarming disease in the Arctic regions. It appears that one great cause of this is the use of improper food, and other carelessness; in fact, that the evil chiefly arises from preventible causes. It is worth while to notice, in this place, the testimony of Scoresby as to the use of stimulants in the Arctic regions. He says: 'Whenever I have had occasion to expose myself to severe cold, I have found that the more I am heated, the longer I can resist the cold without incon-

Ben in the galley making tea for the crew.

Ros preparing breakfast.

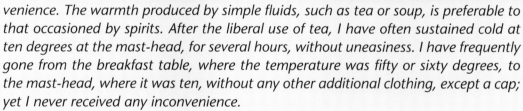

venience. The warmth produced by simple fluids, such as tea or soup, is preferable to that occasioned by spirits. After the liberal use of tea, I have often sustained cold at ten degrees at the mast-head, for several hours, without uneasiness. I have frequently gone from the breakfast table, where the temperature was fifty or sixty degrees, to the mast-head, where it was ten, without any other additional clothing, except a cap; yet I never received any inconvenience.

Left: *Celebrating Denis' birthday with a special meal 6 August 2016.* Above: *Provisions waiting to be stored on board.*

58

BEN'S BLOG
10 July 2016

During my downtime I began to feel sick. Twenty odd minutes before my watch I came and threw up my dinner. Macaroni cheese and strawberry yoghurt all mixed together. It was exactly as bad as it sounds. That night the weather was appalling. Rain, wind, roughish sea, the whole lot. I threw up again and so did Hazel when she came to relieve me. Because of the weather Dave and I developed a system of each person doing 15 minutes on their own before going down below to keep warm and being replaced. When Annie came up she didn't want to go down again, so I spent a lot of time keeping warm.

At sea again after their brief return to Tromsø, Ben and Hazel both feel the effects of the worsening weather as *Northabout* rounds Nordkapp (North Cape), the most northerly point of Europe. Ben had visited the area three years earlier walking to the very tip of the peninsula at Knivshelloden taking in the dramatic view of towering, barren cliffs edging the Arctic Ocean. Now, with a bucket at hand, on a cold and choppy sea the prospect was not quite so alluring and arrival at Vardo could not come too soon.

Their arrival in a bright and sunny Vardo on the morning of 11 July provided a welcome respite. John arrived with the generator parts which Nikolai replaced, while the members of the crew explored the little town, a major fishery centre and reeking of fish, before visiting the museum and catching up on communications with friends and family back home. Here goodbyes are said to Hazel who is heading home.

On 14 July, after an uneventful two day voyage, *Northabout* sails into Murmansk successfully concluding an eventful first leg of Polar Ocean Challenge.

Northabout shelters among the fishing boats at Vardo.

The North East Passage
The Second Leg of the Polar Ocean Challenge

Dave Cushing looks out over the bleak skyline of Murmansk on the morning of 14 July.

THE PORT OF MURMANSK WAS OFFICIALLY FOUNDED in 1916. Its importance lies in it being kept ice free all winter due to the influence of the Gulf Stream making it Russia's natural gateway to the Arctic Ocean. Almost completely destroyed by German bombing during the Second World War the architecture of the rebuilt city is brutalist, seemingly more bleak during its interminable winters, the midnight sun appearing above the horizon for only 63 days annually. The export of coal from here coats the whole place with a thin veil of dust.

Here it's all change as far as *Northabout*'s crew is concerned, Annie, John and Dave Cushing are to leave for home, and David Hempleman-Adams, Constance Difede, Barbara Fitzpatrick and Denis Davydov joining the crew for the next leg.

Despite now having two Russians aboard the port authorities show no sign of relenting in their thoroughgoing bureaucracy, as Ben relates:

We came into Murmansk while I was asleep and woke up when the immigration people came on board. There's something very unsettling about having four people who you don't know, speaking a language you don't understand, getting you to sign lots

Barbara Fitzpatrick and Constance Difede, seasoned travellers and members of the exclusive Explorers Club join Northabout *in Murmansk for the North East and North West Passages.*

Denis Davydov joins the crew in Murmansk – here with Nikolai and Ben. A compatriot of Nikolai's and an experienced sailor and engineer, Denis proved his worth throughout the second and third legs.

of bits of paper that will allow you to stay in their country. It didn't help that one of them was in some kind of military uniform.

After a couple of hours, with Nikolai acting as translator, the customs officers eventually appeared satisfied and Ben was able to step ashore, heading for the hotel where David was staying in order to take advantage of a hot shower and, as always when in port, finding somewhere to eat. Later, tracked down by local newsmen, Ben gives a media interview with Nikolai again acting as translator.

GoPro camera shot of Northabout *manouvreing away from the jetty in Murmansk watched by two Russion dockhands. Nikolai is at the helm, Barbara watching on, Ben on the right and Ros at the bowline.*

With no facilities for visiting yachts, North-about *tied up among the various tugs and merchantmen calling at the port. This photograph shows the massive coal jetties (on the right) the dust from which covers the city in a fine coating.*

Meanwhile David Hempleman-Adams is attempting to progress the granting of permits for the onward journey, without much success. Frustrating for him too is the news coming in from daily ice reports which tantalisingly show open water on the immediate course they would take, although with changes being so unpredictable in the Arctic, planning when to go is creating something of a headache for the expedition leader:

Unquestionably overall we will see less ice but ironically not in the areas we are starting from. In fact the Kara Sea (north of Siberia) which is traditionally full of ice at this time is open. But the Laptev Sea (further east) is solid. Solid right up to the beach. This could be because less multi-year ice means more thinner first year ice which is the stuff that floats with the currents and can block the channels.

At the moment we could speed through the North West Passage now if we could get there. The sea ice there has really receded. Maybe when we do get there it will be frozen again. Such is life! And of course if it was that easy everyone would do it! I find myself with a constant internal conflict. I want clear ice to sail but of course if

DAVID HEMPLEMAN-ADAMS' BLOG
15 July 2016

Ironically whilst the NW passage is now nearly open way ahead of schedule on the North East passage the route is solid ice right up to the land and is the worst for many years. We are trying to predict when to leave as it will take 10 days to get to that point. Will it have changed by then? We don't want to be stuck in the ice waiting. We also don't want to miss an opportunity when we are sat in Murmansk. What to do?

Secondly we arrived with our treasured permit. Now they tell us the rules have changed ! We need a different one and need to open and close it in Providencia which would add 4 days to our trip. At this moment in time I would take it but immigration, customs and coastguard vie for the number of boxes to be ticked.

I do sail around then as we have said it goes to prove that we have real problems with the planet. But I want to succeed in sailing round because in that way the expedition manages to highlight the problem.

With Denis and Nikolai spending most of the time on board making final adjustments to the engine, other crew members are sightseeing and buying provisions for the next leg. Meanwhile Constance and Barbara have used the downtime to take a trip to St Petersburg – tempting for Ros, Ben and his older sister, Bea, who has flown in to Murmansk to share the time with her family, but resisted as they have so much to do, as Ros relates in her blog of 20 July on the eve of sailing:

I am sitting in the reception of the Azimuth Hotel in Murmansk making use of the free wifi to do some last minute emails. We have a safety briefing at 1300 and then we will be going through the immigration and customs procedures ready to leave the port this afternoon.

The last week has been a whirlwind. I have been taking the North East Passage first week's food, and all of the baking and flavouring ingredients, out of the long term storage on the boat and putting them where we can reach them more easily while sailing, as well as trying to clean and organise the living areas while the floors and hatches are up for engineering work, and getting extra supplies in Murmansk – I love the latter, a great way to get to know a city and the people. Barbara and Constance have done an enormous fresh food shop in the Okay supermarket in Murmansk. And Ben and I have been working on a few IT upgrades to try to make sure that we can send photos, recordings and video successfully while we are sailing. Nikolai, our skipper, and his first mate Denis have been fixing engineering problems and making some engineering upgrades to try to make sure that we are in the best possible state for the adventure to come. And David has been negotiating our permits and visas.

This is my first moment for reflection in Murmansk. We have been working from six until midnight most days, with time out for lovely dinners (the food in Murmansk is excellent), and a trip to the Lenin *icebreaker and the Murmansk war memorial with Ben, but otherwise full on.*

BEN'S BLOG
18 July 2016

It's ten pm on Sunday right now and we're still in Murmansk. I got up at about lunchtime again and The Mother and I went out to get out of Nikolai and Denis's ways. They were in the engine again. We went back to the café that does good pizza for breakfast. We tried to order something different this time but the communication problems meant that we ended up having pizza for breakfast/lunch. We had showers in the hotel again and then went to try and find some things we need for the North East Passage. We found a coffee jug thing which we need. We lost the last one, and at long last, we found a supermarket. We packed a lot of egg powder at the start of the trip which has all gone missing. As such all the time we've been in Murmansk we've been trying to find somewhere that sells eggs to supplement the supply. Four days and we've only found one shop that sells eggs. So we got two hundred.

ICEBREAKER

"On arriving at the northern extremity of Nova Zembla, the explorers found the sea so loaded with ice, that Barentz despaired of effecting a passage, and resolved on returning home. The second voyage of Barentz met with signal failure, and the last and most important was undertaken in 1596. Two ships started on the 10th of May and arrived at Nova Zembla on the 17th of July. There the vessel commanded by Barentz was embayed in drifting ice, and the adventurer foresaw something of the horrors of an Arctic winter."

John Tillotson. *Adventures in the Ice*, 1869

Northabout *meets the ice fields.*

With time to do a little exploring of their own, Ben and Ros decide to pay a visit to the world's first nuclear powered icebreaker, NS *Lenin*. Decommissioned in 1989 she now lies in Murmansk as a major tourist attraction and also as an icon of Russian power in the region. With Arctic ice disappearing it's unclear what the future holds for these highly specialist vessels but the Russians are taking no chances and, keen to be at the forefront of Arctic exploitation, they continue to build icebreakers in order to ensure that they can resupply their six military bases, 16 deepwater ports and 13 air bases all within the Arctic Circle. By comparison the USA has only one icebreaker and no major military base north of the Arctic Circle.

From the eleventh century Russian settlers on the shores of the Arctic Ocean have constructed vessels adapted to ice conditions at sea and on frozen rivers. These were called kochi.

With its rounded shape and strong metal hull, the Russian Pilot of 1864 was an important predecessor of modern icebreakers with a propeller. Its curved bow allowed the vessel to push herself on the top of the ice and consequently break it. Here she's commemorated on a postage stamp.

Ben in the captain's chair aboard NS Lenin.

Built at the end of the 19th century the Russian naval icebreaker SS Ermark approaches Kronstadt. The original caption read 'On her first trip she cut her way through solid ice, leaving behind her a broad channel in the desert of ice. Here the people gather to witness the arrival of the vessel and drive alongside in sledges.'

Control room aboard NS Lenin.

One of Russia's newest and largest of her forty icebreakers, the NS50 Let Pobedy.

While Ben explores the vast interior of NS *Lenin*, David and Nikolai visit some of the Russian's friends on the outskirts of the city:

Last night I went to a small dacha (Russian second home), outside Murmansk and met friends of Nikolai. They worked on the ice breakers so were keen to pass on help and information. What is the common theme here is whatever the ice maps show it can all change quickly if we get a southerly wind for a couple of days blowing the pack ice offshore. Today we're ready to go, so welcome home sea sickness, no change of clothes, wet watches, sleeping in a tumble drier and the smell of adventure!

The truth is that waiting for permits and indecision regarding the state of the ice ahead has begun to take its toll on the crew, Ben among them, who have had enough of shore life and need to get back to sea. And so, on 21 July, *Northabout* sails from her unprepossessing berth and heads towards the sea. The weather is warm and under a blue sky they sail past the rusting hulks of abandoned icebreakers and, leaving Murmansk's massive naval base in their wake, they head out into the Barents Sea.

It doesn't take long for the crew to get down to the routines of life on board, Constance making the most of Ros's provisions by conjuring up a pasta supper with three kinds of cheese! The sighting of a whale puts the final touch to the day as the sun dips to the horizon and the crew prepare for sleep.

Opposite: Dealing with ice aboard North-about whose icebreaking abilities the crew were reluctant to put to the test. On entering a field of surface ice it's vital to assess its extent and to avoid become ice-bound. Here, while one or more members of the crew stand at the bow to ease ice away from the sides of the vessel, Denis climbs the mast to warn Ben at the helm about ice ahead and to spot for leads that will allow clear passage. This called for skill and complete co-ordination among the crew.

BEN'S BLOG
18 July 2016

For the past few days we've been in a place that, while interesting, is not very, stimulating. We've been working to get the boat ready, I don't understand the local language, the city's design is frankly oppressive and all in all the experience is right now very tiring. I am, for want of a better term, jaded. I am certain this will change with a change of scenery and when we actually get under way. But right now, everything feels a bit worn, sort of twilight zoneish.

The midnight sun sits on the horizon as Northabout *enters the Barents Sea heading for the North East Passage.*

SECOND LEG
Murmansk-Cape Barrow

POLAR OCEAN
CHALLENGE

After spending a week in Murmansk, on 21 July, Northabout starts out on the longest leg of the PoC with Cape Barrow, Alaska, at the end of a 5000 mile voyage. Yet uncertainty hangs over the likelihood of success as the ice charts show the way ahead completely blocked by ice at Cape Chelyuskin preventing their entry into the Laptev Sea and beyond. The map shows the zig-zag line above Novaya Zemlya as Northabout tacks, first north then east, waiting for news of ice and wind forecasts before entering the Kara Sea.

The good weather continues the following day although an increasing chill heralds their northward progress. It had been agreed to keep *Northabout* under sail for as much of the second and third legs as possible in order to conserve fuel for the engine should they be forced to motor when navigating through ice, and Nikolai uses this period of good sailing weather to ensure the crew are familiar with helming the vessel without the aid of the autopilot – a wise precaution in the event of an electronic failure – and an opportunity for Ben to put into further practice the lessons learned on his RYA courses in Suffolk.

David and Nikolai spend hours poring over the ice charts that are arriving regularly over the satellite link. And it turned out that the visit to the dacha was not merely a social occasion it was also a chance for Nikolai to meet up with an old friend, Sergei, who worked for a Murmansk shipping company and is responsible for providing tankers and icebreakers daily ice and weather reports. These up-to-the-minute charts allowed Nikolai more accurately to predict the ice ahead and navigate *Northabout*'s course through the North East Passage.

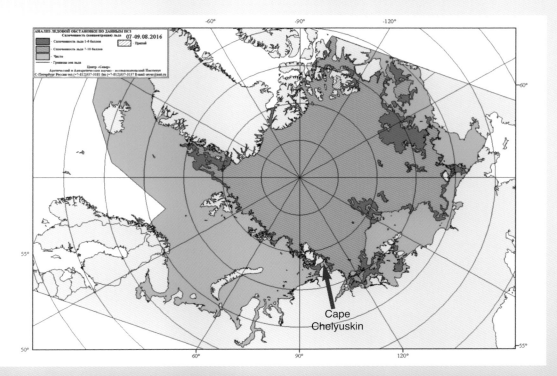

Russian ice chart showing the extent of ice across Northabout's intended route through the North East Passage. The relative depth of the ice is shown in orange (polar ice) and green (sea ice) and at Cape Chelyuskin (marked with a green arrow) the ice is impassable.

The aim was to sail from Murmansk north-east into the Barents Sea to Novaya Zemlya where they would pass north of that archipelago and then into the Kara Sea, the Laptev Sea and the East Siberian Sea, hugging the coast wherever possible, hoping the ice, currently blocking the route at Cape Chelyuskin, had retreated far enough towards the pole to allow passage. These uncertainties and the prospect of entering the unknown perils of the North East Passage are reflected on in Ros Edwards' blog of the first day at sea – thoughts shared no doubt by others on board:

So what will it be like? Will the ice clear to let us through in time for the subsequent legs to make it the whole way round in one season? Will the victualling be good enough that we can prepare what I have bought while sailing for 24 hours a day, even in rough weather, and everyone can eat well and stay happy and healthy – my responsibility and it feels huge, although trivial compared with David's and Nikolai's responsibilities.

And what will it be like? How does it feel to be surrounded by an icy ocean, making slow progress and picking a way through. I am especially excited about this and can't really imagine it. So, now I am ready to get going and to see what is in store for us. Briefing at 1300, and had better take the seasickness pills…

The last spit of land at the end of the channel leaving Murmansk. Ben and David enjoy the relative warmth of the sun and a calm sea.

Ros celebrates with a little Russian 'Happy Birthday' cake presented by crewmates Denis and Nikolai.

BEN'S BLOG
22 July 2016

We had a little birthday party for The Mother. She got three cakes, some chocolates, a T-shirt from Nikolai's yacht and and a little pot she'd chosen from me. We still have most of the cake. Two are a sort of heavy Russian cake with raspberry jam in the middle. The third reminds me of an opera cake. They're very nice.

One of the dolphins I saw today was a bit odd. It would leap out of the water and then turn onto its back and crash back down into the water. I have no idea why. In any case, it was funny. I'm surprised at the number of dolphins we're seeing. And all of them seem to be going east.

The following day, the 22nd, the fair weather continues and the crew join Ros in celebrating her birthday aboard. As if to celebrate too, a pod of dolphins appears in the turquoise sea, swimming alongside *Northabout* as they head north-east under sail, next waypoint being the archipelago of Novaya Zemlya about four days' distant.

But from T shirts in Murmansk it's now trawler suit, Primaloft and fleece time, with both air and water temperatures dropping rapidly.

Mother and son on watch and well wrapped up as Northabout heads north-east towards Novaya Zemlya. Shot from the GoPro.

70

Along with daily written blogs, Ben sends back audio blogs for uploading to the Wicked Weather Watch and PoC websites with feedback coming in from individual followers, friends and family back home. Keeping this as a regular thing is not easy as times passes differently in these higher latitudes as Ben relates:

The thing is, because you're 24 hour sailing, you're awake at all hours, except those that you'd normally be awake for. You also have twenty-four-hour daylight. This means that you have no measure for time passing. You get up at twelve at night to go the toilet and its exactly the same as twelve noon. The only difference I've noticed is that at night it's colder. This means that my main indicator for time passing is how runny my nose is. This is not a joke.

No joke either is the discipline aboard relating to crew safety as *Northabout* sails closer to the ice fields:

Over the past few days the weather has been getting progressively colder. Air temperature is about six degrees, water temperature is only two degrees higher. Fall in here and even if you are rescued you will almost certainly die of hypothermia. Fun! Because of the risk of falling overboard we all have lifejackets that have built in harnesses. We then have cords that we attach to various points around the boat so that if we do get thrown around we don't go in the drink. David has insisted on a policy of, whenever you're on deck you have you're lifejacket on and are clipped in. I know this is the wrong attitude for a teenager to take but I wouldn't have it any other way.

Barbara.

Taking no chances. Ben on morning watch, suited and booted and well clipped in.

BEN'S BLOG
24 July 2016

I managed to get Barbara to do an audio blog for the BBC Today program today. As it turns out she's very good at that sort of thing. It was quite a short one but in my opinion much better than the ones even David has been doing. Barbara disagrees, here's Barbara now:

"This is the problem with sitting next to Ben when he is doing his blog! He is very persuasive, has been chasing me for days to do an audio blog and eventually today we got around to doing the Tascam recording, of course, I like most people, don't like the sound of my voice, or at least most of the crew here on Northabout, don't like our own voices. I have tried bribing him to delete or at least cut short the audio blog but he has it all on record now and has threatened to send it to Radio Dublin... such a ratbag! Still... I can now mention his smelly socks!"

POLAR OCEAN CHALLENGE

As they approach the northern tip of Novaya Zemlya heading into the Kara Sea, along with the falling temperatures the sea also starts to change in character, taking on a more sombre aspect, the blue and turquoise turning to a leaden grey under lowering skies. The weather charts for 25 July predict an increase in wind speed and the ice charts show no sign of the ice retreating to allow passage past Cape Chelyuskin.

Ironically, the winds so far had allowed rapid progress under sail, conserving fuel for possible difficulties in the ice later on, but now, finding themselves fast approaching the vast open waters of the dangerous Kara Sea they are forced to tack, first north, then east, hoping the forecasts improve. For David and Nikolai these conditions present a dilemma, press on or seek shelter – a problem David sums up in his blog for the 26th:

So, we need to get through the straight and through the Laptev Sea. So where do we wait until we can do this? We have deliberately taken our time to get to this point, and used the wind as much as we can to conserve fuel. There is no hurry. We will slowly make our way east, and if we can find an island with no fast ice around, will look for a sheltered spot, until we get better ice conditions. The other options are to heave to and wait, but this is a sailing yacht, she needs to sail. And if we get a southerly blow, it could change our chances very quickly to get around, so we need to be close to react.

What followed is not quite what David had in mind.

The bleak low outline of Novaya Zemlya.

MAN OVERBOARD!

In the autumn of 2014 *Northabout* had been sailed from Ireland to the boatyard in Sharpness on the River Severn where a major refit was to take place. The extent of this work delayed the original intended start date of the Polar Ocean Challenge at midsummer 2015 and, instead, it was decided to try out the vessel on a shakedown cruise to Svalbard with Ben and his parents as part of the crew. While *Northabout* performed well, her sea trails revealed a number of issues that needed to be fixed before facing the sterner test in circumnavigating the Pole. For Steve and Ros Edwards, safety was a paramount consideration in undertaking the Polar Ocean Challenge, not least as their 14-year-old son was to be on board. Expedition leader, David Hempleman-Adams, while anxious to get the Polar Ocean Challenge underway, recognised he had a duty of care towards those who were to attempt the Challenge:

Later on, after the Spitsbergen trip, such concerns as I may have had regarding the boat were alleviated by the firm and experienced hand of Steve Edwards. Steve had already expressed an interest in joining the Polar Ocean Challenge along with his wife and family and quite naturally wanted to ensure that Northabout *would provide the safest possible vessel for that undertaking. An experienced sailor, Steve suggested we employ Colin Walker of Walker Planning & Construction to oversee the refitting of Northabout in preparation for the main voyage following our return from Spitsbergen. Steve's intervention was a godsend to me as it relieved me of any concerns over the* Northabout*'s seaworthiness and allowed time for me to track down the best possible skipper for sailing in polar waters.*

Ben helming on Northabout *in rough seas.*

SURVIVAL SUIT

Hood

Wave Shield

Velcro face shield

Whistle pocket

Light pocket

Waist belt

Watertight zip

Gloves

Reflective tape

Ankle strap

Boots

Ben at the helm wearing a padded safety harness and securely clipped on.

Along with sorting out niggles in the fuel system and a complete overhaul of the vessel's electronics, further attention was paid to *Northabout's* safety equipment. To this end Colin installed a liferaft bracket on the transom to secure an inflatable 10-man liferaft, for which two 15hp outboards were purchased. The inflatable also served as a tender and could be used for pulling the boat away from ice if needed.

Stowed for use in an emergency were survival suits (immersion suits), one for each crew member, to be donned as a last resort should the situation arise. These are body-covering suits worn specifically for the purpose of remaining afloat and surviving during emergencies in high seas. They are generally made from neoprene, which has the property to withstand extreme temperatures of water and is fire retardant. The immersion suit covers the person's body without exposing any part to the water. It also has a protective hood to cover the head.

On *Northabout* during the Polar Ocean Challenge there was only one occasion when it became necessary for the crew to don their suits, this during a storm in the Laptev Sea. Not so with the crew's safety harnesses which were worn whenever on watch on deck and at the helm, instinctively clipping the tether on to a nearby jackline or padeye.

Sailing in Arctic waters brings particular perils for those who find themselves thrown into the sea. In the past, without the benefit of high-tech clothing and sophisticated search and rescue techniques, anyone finding themselves in the icy seas for more than a few minutes was unlikely to survive. The strategies for dealing with such casualties is now more sophisticated but for those taking part in the Arctic convoys during the Second World War it was not so much the fear or enemy bombs and torpedoes that occupied their minds, but the prospect of having to abandon ship in those bleak and freezing seas. On 16 April 1942, the SS *Empire Howard*, carrying war supplies from the Tyne to Murmansk was torpedoed off the Iceland coast, the surface water temperature at -2°C. Her Captain, H.J.M. Downie, takes up the story:

I was the last man to be picked up at 1400. Everyone was conscious when taken out of the water but many of the men lost consciousness when taken into the warmth of the trawlers. Nine of the men died soon after being picked up. We were all given a small mouthful of spirits and this made us sleep, and these unfortunate men went to sleep and did not wake up again.

Experienced sailors know that drifting ice is a constant peril, moving at surprising speed under tides and winds. Large chunks batter the sides of a vessel and accumulate as dead weight around anchor chains when moored. Falling overboard amongst floating ice provides additional dangers to both victim and would-be rescuers.

THE EFFECTS ON THE BODY OF IMMERSION IN WATER AS CORE TEMPERATURE DROPS

Temp °C	EFFECT
33	body temperature regulation fails.
32.2	shivering response ceases, muscular rigidity begins, speech become difficult.
31-29	drowsiness occurs
29	unconsciousness occurs
25	death occurs

Seeking advice from some seasoned Russian sailors while *Northabout* stopped over near Murmansk, David Hempleman Adams recalled: 'What they impressed upon me was, that whatever the ice charts showed, the situation at sea could change rapidly. A southerly wind could blow the pack ice offshore leaving a seaway open that hours before had not existed.'

Fridtjof Nansen, describes a terrifying incident in the *Fram* expedition of 1893–96, during the fifteen month journey he and Hjalmar Johansen spent crossing the Arctic ice by sledge carrying supplies and kayaks. In March 1895, with *Fram* icebound, the two men set out to attempt to reach the North Pole some 350 miles distant. Thwarted by the southerly drift of the ice which took them ever further from their goal, by June, as the ice broke up, they were forced to retreat towards Franz Josef Land, using their kayaks to cross open water. One evening they made camp on a large floe, tying up the kayaks alongside:

Johansen suddenly cried, "I say! the kayaks are adrift!" We ran down as hard as we could. They were already a little way out, and were drifting quickly off; the painter had given way. "Here, take my watch!" I said to Johansen, giving it to him; and as quickly as possible I threw off some clothing, so as to be able to swim more easily. I did not dare to take everything off, as I might so easily get cramp. I sprang into the water, but the wind was off the ice, and the light kayaks, with their high rigging, gave it a good hold. They were already well out, and were drifting rapidly. The water was icy cold; it was hard work swimming with clothes on; and the kayaks drifted farther and farther, often quicker than I could swim.

PREDICTED SURVIVAL TIMES FOR THOSE IMMERSED IN WATER WITHOUT SURVIVAL SUITS	
Water Temp °C	MAXIMUM TIME FOR SURVIVAL
0	¼ hour
2.5	½ hour
5	1 hour
10	3 hours
15	7 hours
20	16 hours

Hjalmar Johansen.

A frozen Nansen struggles aboard the kayaks with the last remaining ounce of his strength.

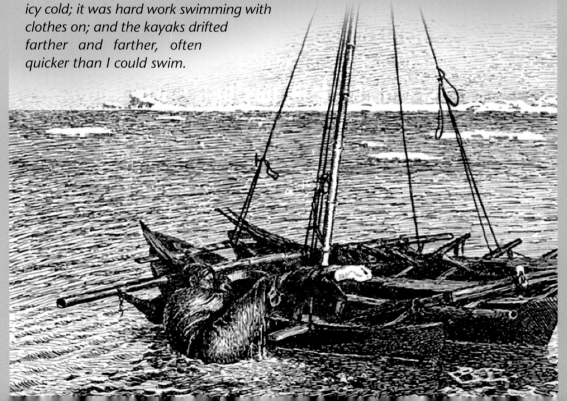

It seemed more than doubtful whether I could manage it. But all our hope was drifting there; all we possessed was on board – we had not even a knife with us; and whether I got cramp and sank here, or turned back without the kayaks, it would come to pretty much the same thing; so I exerted myself to the utmost... I felt, however, that my limbs were gradually stiffening and losing all feeling, and I knew that in a short time I should not be able to move them... At last I was able to stretch out my hand to the snow-shoe which lay across the sterns. I grasped it, pulled myself in to the edge of the kayak – and we were saved!

In his book *Eskimo Life*, published in 1894, Nansen describes in detail the skills of the native people of the Arctic in building and sailing kayaks, These superbly crafted vessels provided the principal means by which these remote peoples hunted seal, walrus and narwhal from which much of their food and material possessions was derived. Although still in use today most kayaks have been replaced by modern motorised inflatables and glass fibre boats.

Nansen also illustrates how well protected the eskimo were from the freezing waters, their clothing made entirely from seal skins, the traditional equivalent of the high-tech wind and waterproof clothing worn by the crew of *Northabout*.

Fridtjof Nansen.

In fair weather the kaiak-man uses the so-called half-jacket (akuilisak). This is made of water-tight skin with the hair removed, and is sewn with sinews. Round its lower margin runs a draw-string, or rather a draw-thong, by means of which the edge of the jacket can be made to fit so closely to the kaiak-ring that it can only be pressed and drawn down over it with some little trouble. This done, the half-jacket forms, as it were, a water-tight extension of the kaiak. The upper margin of the jacket comes close up to the armpits of the kaiak-man, and is supported by braces or straps, which pass over the shoulders and can be lengthened or shortened by means of handy runners or buckles of bone, so simple and yet so ingenious that we, with all our metal buckles and so forth, cannot equal them. Loose sleeves of skin are drawn over the arms, and are lashed to the over-arm and to the wrist, thus preventing the arm from becoming wet. Watertight mittens of skin are drawn over the hands.

This half-jacket is enough to keep out the smaller waves which wash over the kaiak. In a heavier sea, on the other hand, the whole-jacket (tuilik) is used. This is made in the same way as the half-jacket, and, like it, fits close to the kaiak-ring, but is longer above, has sleeves attached to it, and a hood which comes right over the head. It is laced tight round the face and wrists, so that with it on the kaiak-man can go right through the breakers and can capsize and right himself again, without getting wet and without letting a drop of water into the kaiak.

Kayaker's half-jacket.

Kayaker's whole-jacket.

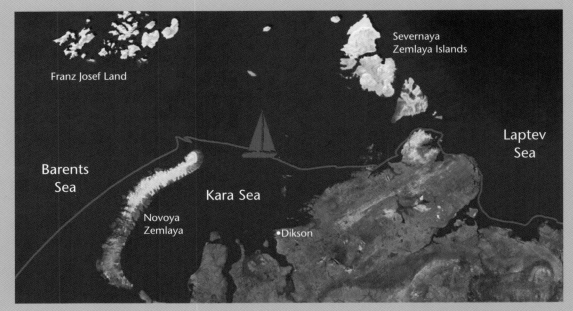

Northabout's position in the Kara Sea at the time the storm hit on 28 July.

BEN'S BLOG
28 July 2016

David was helming when the weather reached its peak. We approached a huge wave and as it filled the portholes' views the boat come crashing down. We braced for it to rock back up, it didn't. The swell was too high and we didn't go over. The wave came over the foredeck, the saloon, the cockpit. We're engulfed and for a second, the entire boat was consumed by the massive body of water. That second passed and the water roared off the decks as we plummeted into the trough on the other side. Water had come through in a dozen places: vents, the companionway and poorly sealed windows. But that was not my concern, I grabbed the cover of the companionway, pulled it back and breathed a sigh of relief. David was still there. Water would dry and we could place back any objects that had come loose but with a wave of that size the main danger was that David had been washed over while helming. True, I knew he was clipped in but all that really meant was that he could be being dragged behind the boat rather than be fully detached. As luck would have it he'd been positioned so that he was braced against such an assault.

For Ben and his fellow crew members two significant storms were encountered during the four-month voyage. The first of these came two weeks after sailing from Murmansk, heading eastwards off the coast of Russia at the end of July. Having slipped past the northern tip of the archipelago of Novoya Zemlya and into the Kara Sea, the weather charts showed *Northabout* heading into a storm. David Hempleman Adams takes up the story:

If we hadn't known it before, by 28 July we were beginning to realise the serious nature of our adventure. Winds had increased to 7 or 8 on the Beaufort scale, gale force with attendant white-crested waves throwing spindrift and spray over Northabout's reeling deck. No one ventured outside and the violent movement inside the boat prevented any sort of activity other than the essentials. Everyone was warned to wear their safety gear and clip on during watches... On the morning of the 28th I'd crawled out of bed, finding my sea legs under Northabout's rocking and rolling, shivering as I got dressed and deciding to put my second thermals. After a quick check of the log I clipped on before leaving the saloon and again as I took over the helm, bracing myself behind the wheel. Sitting down, I put my leg up for stability just as a huge wave came across the boat. I hadn't seen its approach and was taken completely by surprise. For a fraction of a second, my whole body was under water, and it was only my leg stopping me going overboard. As the wave cleared in a cascade of water racing over the side, I emerged with a mouthful of seawater, spouting like a goldfish in a Disney cartoon.

For Ben and the rest of *Northabout*'s crew their first taste of an Arctic storm, as dramatic as it had been, was also an episode in which their collective spirit and expertise as sailors had been tested and shown to be up to the challenge of the voyage ahead. A general atmosphere of satisfaction suffused the hours following the storm and David's blog of the events summed up his feelings: 'The crew were brilliant today. Some say they were petrified, but still got on the helm'.

For Ben, watches during the storm resulted in a face covered with a layer of dried salt – and worse:

I have a cold. It's my fault of course. Yesterday on my first half hour of the horrible watch I had no hat and had my hood pulled back so that I could see better. A wave came over the side and hit my in the face, that was, to put it mildly, cold. A couple of hours after that I developed a blocked nose, headache and sore throat. This got progressively worse as the day went on and I spent the night with little sleep. The morning came and the cold was a little better. I still couldn't breathe through my nose though and the headache was not exactly fun. We've been able to go more or less due east since this morning. I have to admit that this bit of the journey has been very Twilight Zone-like. I have completely lost track of time, as has everyone else I think. I'm really looking forward to getting to some land and hopefully some shelter from the wind. And the waves actually, no waves would be lovely. This blog is going to be very short I've afraid, this is because I'm currently finding thinking very difficult, probably because of the cold, as in the virus not the temperature!

Denis reefing the mainsail before the storm hits.

DAVID HEMPLEMAN-ADAMS' BLOG
28 July 2016

Last couple of days have been interesting. Great thing about modern weather charts, you can predict what's going to happen. We were in for a couple of days of stormy weather. I was taught to get a reef in before you need it, the Russians believe put a reef in when you need it, subtle difference. In the end, we put all three in.

A waveswept and windswept Ben at the helm with the seas rising behind him, seen from the GoPro camera. Around this time the autopilot stopped working and so everyone had to take turns at the helm.

Pack ice stretching out on the horizon, Nikolai suggests the way forward to Barbara at the helm.

BEN'S BLOG
30 July 2016

ICE! We came across ice today! Or at least so I'm told, I was in bed. It was after my watch, about eleven thirty, as far as I know we were just sailing along and a small chunk of ice floated by. This is exciting for two reasons: one, we're getting close to the pack ice which means we're getting through the journey and two, we're approaching land again, according to Nikolai we should be in a little bay on a island safely out of the wind by midnight. This means we'll have a few hours or days to rest, make repairs and generally enjoy not being tossed around by the waves. Not long now, I can't wait. Just now I noticed land off the starboard side. It's very faint and there's not much of it but it's definitely land which means we're definitely close to land which is the most exciting thing thats happened all week.

Then, on 30 July what the whole crew had been waiting for – Ice! At first almost invisible, a thin veil on the surface of the water, the broad white bands of floating ice spread across the sea ahead as *Northabout* approached. This again lifted the mood on the boat for this drifting ice signalled that the recent storms had begun to shift the ice offshore, possibly opening up the route ahead.

This resulted in renewed interest in poring over the daily ice charts with Nikolai and Denis making bets with each other as to when the Vilkitsky (Vilkitskogo) Strait that lies off Cape Chelyuskin and forms the entrance to the Laptev Sea would eventually be ice free; Nikolai putting his money on 9 August (his birthday) and Denis on the 6th (his own), in less than a week's time. The remainder of the crew, Ben particularly, were rather more interested in the immediate prospect of reaching the little island group that lay ahead where Nikolai had suggested they lay up in the meantime.

In a quieter moment Ros records a video diary to camera describing the dramas of the past few days, remarking on Ben's handling of Northabout *during the storm.*

BEN'S BLOG
31 July 2016

Today at seven o'clock exactly we sailed into a sheltered bay in the middle of an archipelago just west of a passage made up of three islands, that is where the proper ice starts. It is a huge relief. We've been sailing non stop for the last eleven days and though you don't really notice it during the journey twenty-four hour travel really grinds you down. Inside this bay we have almost no wind and absolutely no swell. The boat is level for the first time in two weeks and I can lie flat in my bunk. The surrounding area is very familiar. It's basically Scotland. Low brown bleak moors with bits of jutting rock here and there. There is some ice about but it's mainly on the low rocky beaches that are dotted about everywhere. We haven't done much after anchoring. Mostly we've just been sitting around and enjoying not moving for a few hours. Lots of effort was put into dinner this evening. We brought a set of pizza bases that we got out and made pizzas with.

And so on the last day of July *Northabout* is guided towards the cove by Nikolai who has been here before. Lots of the islands in this region are named after Russian ice pilots and this one is called Pilot Makhotkina. The crew call their new home the 'Blue Lagoon' and it's well named for, although arriving under sullen skies the weather steadily improves.

The Nordenshel'da (Nordensköld) Archipelago comprises a cluster of islands west of Cape Chelyuskin. Here Northabout *finds a safe haven inside a sheltered cove (yellow dot) for eight days from 31 July. The crew name the cove their 'Blue Lagoon'.*

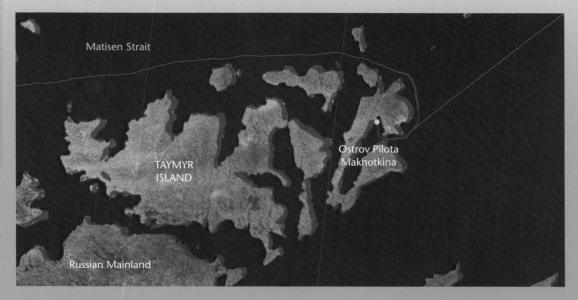

Matisen Strait

TAYMYR
ISLAND

Ostrov Pilota
Makhotkina

Russian Mainland

Here, after a few hours recovery, everyone on board has a job to do, from general maintenance of the engine, chart plotter, generator and oven to cleaning up below decks and getting personal washing done. In her blog of 2 August, Ros takes a moment to reflect on the past few days:

This will be our third day at anchor in a beautiful isolated island, tucked deep in its heart through a winding channel, putting us out of the way of the worst of the sea and wind. We have had two glorious days of sun and comparative warmth. Time for Nikolai and Denis to do essential remedial work on the boat. And for the rest of us to recover from twenty-four-hour sailing, which is peculiarly gruelling. Its not just the shift patterns of watches and chores we keep, but before we anchored here we had a particularly uncomfortable time in a big gale, where the safest place was to be in our bunks unless we were helming (because the autopilot wasn't coping).

So, safest place in our bunks...?! Well, I am lucky to have a roomy bunk, but this also means that if it's rough I can get rolled around my cabin and end up in the footwell by the bunk. Or in one of the storage cubby holes! I have developed methods of packing luggage and my survival suit around my bunk, and lying tucked up across the bunk, with my knees against one side and shoulders against the other, which seems to keep me more or less in one place!

Everyone has slightly different challenges with their watch patterns and sleeping arrangements. Constance has a 0200 to 0600 watch which personally I think must

Ben brings Northabout *through the entrance into the Blue Lagoon.*

Evening in the Blue Lagoon.

The somewhat cramped quarters below deck.

BARBARA FITZPATRICK'S BLOG
2 August 2016
Nordenshel'da Archipelago

It's Tuesday afternoon and we have been at anchor since Sunday morning in a beautiful bay off the coast of Siberia. We have had blue skies and the sun has beamed down on us, this little bay has been the perfect oasis for Northabout *and crew to rest, recuperate and carry out necessary minor odd jobs. There is an eerie silence and calmness here, something to relish after the deafening noise onboard whilst thrashing around at sea. Whilst here, I have so enjoyed solitary moments up on deck absorbing the peace and quiet, feeling the magic of the remoteness and natural beauty surrounding and protecting us.*

be the absolute worst. She also has a similar bunk to mine and on one rough night was actually thrown out of her bunk. Three times. Barbara sleeps in what she describes, fairly accurately, as a shoebox. Luckily she is petite. And Ben has a top bunk tucked right under the cabin roof, with a low side – he has a spare mattress which he tucks down the side of his bunk, making his sleeping space tiny but preventing him from being thrown out of the bunk.

But their new haven was not entirely without alarms. A strengthening wind had blown ice into the anchorage which, as it passed, clanked against *Northabout*'s hull and threatened damage to the anchor chain. This resulted in Denis standing on the bow poling away ice as it passed.

And greaters scares were just around the corner (literally) after it was decided to give the RIB a run out and pay the island a visit.

A Dangerous Haven

Sun 31 July, 2016 South Kara Sea, N.76.16 E.096.56 Pilota Makhotkina

After the trials of crossing the Kara Sea and enduring Force 7 to 8 gales both *Northabout* and her crew were in need of rest and a chance to check over the vessel to repair any damage sustained by the heavy weather. Having passed the rugged coastline of Russia's Taymyr Peninsula they found the perfect place to anchor alongside the island of Ostrova Pilota Makhotkina, which the weary crew called the 'Blue Lagoon'. This low lying spit of land reminded Ben of some of the smaller Scottish islands, featureless and largely unremarkable, although he, as much as any of the crew, welcomed the respite from the constant rolling of the vessel while at sea.

This quiet anchorage and the increasing balmy weather also provided an opportunity for testing the both the GoPro camera and the vessel's RIB, the rubber dinghy that would serve as a life raft in an emergency.

At Anchor in the 'Blue Lagoon'

While the rest of the crew watched from the deck, Nikolai and Ben zoomed around in the RIB (Rigid Inflatable Boat), everyone taking photos and, while Denis decided to try fishing from *Northabout*'s bow, the remaining crew, except for David and the fisherman, thought this would be a good moment to get their land legs back. The RIB drew alongside and they all climbed in (no easy task), heading for the island.

Above: *Ben and Nikolai giving the RIB a work-out.*

Right: *Ben anticipating an hour or two on dry land.*

Below: *Nikolai, Constance and Barbara look back at Northabout anchored in the Blue Lagoon. She seemed very distant, even more so when the bears appeared.*

Arctic poppies are one of the most northerly growing plants in the world. Covered in black hair they are hardy and tough, with some surprisingly delicate yellow or white petals. These flowers continually turn to face the sun, tracking its progress across the sky, and attracting insects to the centre of the bloom. As the climate warms certain species will proliferate while others, adapted solely for Arctic conditions, are likely to decline.

BEARS!

BEN'S BLOG
8 August

"I shouted "Bears!" a couple of times in case anyone hadn't noticed or needed any encouragement to get back to the dinghy!"

After lunch we put the dinghy in the water. Nikolai and I got in and raced around the boat a bit, Nikolai at the helm and me with a GoPro. Once we got back to the boat The Mother, Barbara and Constance got in and we went ashore. There's a shallow beach in the north of the bay we're in without any big rocks that we beached the dingy on and got out of. We walked up and down the beach a little and then we all went up to a little cairn a few dozen metres up a hill, took a few pictures and then started walking back to the boat. Once we were back on the beach The Mother looked over onto the other side of the bay and said, "Thats a polar bear!"

My head snapped round to where she'd been looking and I saw three white dots not too far away moving in our direction. and then ran along the beach to the tender quickly followed by everyone else. Once in the water we were basically safe. The mother wouldn't want to leave her cubs and with the outboard we could move faster through the water than the bear could. We skirted the coast at a safe distance and took pictures. We didn't get too close to the shore because you shouldn't get too close to wildlife in case you disturb it.

Also the bear would try to eat us, there was that also!

Described as 'climate refugees' polar bears, wander close to settlements, scavenging on rubbish tips as their natural food becomes scarce.

Polar Bears are not the only Arctic animals that are threatened by global warming but because they are the most iconic much of the world's attention is given over to their endangerment. They are natural killers, the largest carnivores on earth, and are fantastically well adapted to living on the sea ice. Trouble is, for them their world is literally melting around them and they are being forced to swim greater distances in search of their prey, mainly seals and walruses. Consequently many young bears are dying of starvation.

BEARS!

A MOTHER...

...AND HER CUBS

WE BEAT A HASTY RETRE BACK TO THE NORTHABO

> "Whilst it is pleasing to see a reaffirmed commitment to the Paris Agreement, this should be seen as the very minimum in our responsibility to the environment. This was a missed opportunity to commit to introducing a 25 Year Plan for our environment and it failed to protect the world's most iconic wildlife..."
>
> Lang Banks of the World Wildlife Fund following the Queen's Speech in Parliament, June 2017

Luckily for the crew of *Northabout* the bear and her cubs were spotted early by Ben's mother, Ros, and their boat was at hand. The fact that the island was largely free of snow and ice made the animals easier to see for they are brilliantly camouflaged against their natural environment. An adult bear can run at 40kmph too – on ice even Usain Bolt might be in trouble.

WICKED WEATHER WATCH

The Wicked Weather Watch charity was set up to provide clarity for children and young people about climate change and global warming. It's no coincidence that the polar bear was chosen as the main part of the logo. Check out: https://wickedweatherwatch.org.uk

Don't try this at home! The teenage Horatio Nelson (actually the same age as Ben when he sailed on the Polar Ocean Challenge) attempts to fell a polar bear with the butt of his musket, although this depiction (from a painting by Richard Westall) is pretty fanciful.

One of the most famous encounters with a polar bear – and relevant to *Northabout*'s voyage, was that of a young Horatio Nelson while on the 1773 expedition aboard HMS *Carcass* to attempt the North West Passage. Determined to shoot a bear in order to take its skin home as a present for his father, Nelson took a small boat out to an ice floe and confronted the animal only for his musket to misfire. Cannon fire from the ship, frightening the bear away, saving the nation's future hero.

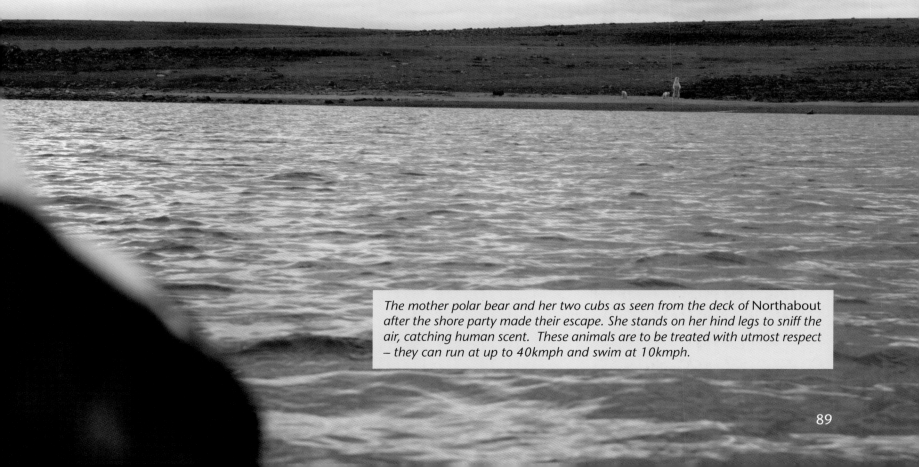

"Ben and Nikolai are the first to have some fun, zigzagging about the bay, with Ben using the GoPro camera to capture shots of Northabout as they whizz past her. Then some bright spark suggested a group outing to the island and so everyone, except for Denis and I, climbed aboard the tender for a spot of sightseeing ashore. I suggested to Denis that this might be the time to break out the Beluga caviar and I was just about to take my first mouthful when, out of the corner of my eye, I caught a movement on the island. Where I half expected to see Nikolai and the gang walking along the shore, there was something altogether more alarming! A large female polar bear was padding along the shoreline with two cubs trotting along in her wake. Luckily, the shore party had seen her too and were now making for the tender. A hungry bear is not to be trifled with, and though it was unlikely she'd leave her cubs, it was a good thing to see everyone back on board, even if it did spoil my and Denis' sneaky feast."

David Hempleman-Adams aboard Northabout 8 August 2016

The mother polar bear and her two cubs as seen from the deck of Northabout after the shore party made their escape. She stands on her hind legs to sniff the air, catching human scent. These animals are to be treated with utmost respect – they can run at up to 40kmph and swim at 10kmph.

Along with testing the RIB, Ben took the opportunity – within the quiet anchorage – also to practice flying the camera drone, brought along as a navigational tool for the moment they reach the serious ice fields that lie ahead:

Ros had the tricky task of catching the drone as it returned to the deck.

Because we're still and we've got some time we decided to put the drone up. That was a nerve wracking experience. I'm the only one on the boat at the moment who can fly the drone so of course it's also my job to make sure it's alright and get it out. So we went onto the deck and cleared an area of ropes and anything that might impede the drone and then I took off. The reason we have the drone is that it is far more accurate to actually see the ice in front of us than be told what the conditions are by the forecast, and it will help us to pick a route through the ice. The drone can climb to about a kilometre I think and can go more than that away from the boat in any one direction. Because of this when we're going along we'll be able to send it up and see whether we need to divert from our current course. The reason I'm worried about this is I don't think I'm a good enough pilot and if I mess up and put it in the water we've got no drone, and if I mess up and put it too close to someone they'll lose a couple of fingers. This is a real risk because the top of the boat is small enough that it is easier to get someone to catch the drone rather than put it on the deck. So no pressure. Anyway, I put it up and flew about a bit and everything was fine. Then the time came to put it back on the boat. That took a long time. What you do as soon as you get the drone in the air is you get it higher than anything that it could possibly crash into, so it was about thirty metres up. I brought the drone down to a couple of metres above sea level and flew it very slowly back to the boat where The Mother was waiting to catch it, wearing very thick gloves of course. I got it over the boat and she grabbed it.

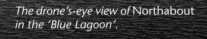

The drone's-eye view of Northabout in the 'Blue Lagoon'.

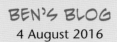

On 6 August the crew celebrate Denis's his birthday but, entertaining as the day was, fuelled by a great deal of vodka, after a week in the cove the crew were itching to move on and the anticipation of the daily ice charts arriving became a focus for everyone's attention – would the ice ahead have shifted sufficiently to allow passage into the Laptev Sea? All the crew blogs from this time speak of how far they have come on this wonderful journey, yet how frustrating it would be not to be able to get further.

Finally, on 8 August, *Northabout* sails out of her anchorage and heads east for the Vilkitsky Strait and Cape Chelyuskin. While the ice charts show the route still blocked, Nikolai believes that the forecast southerly winds will shift the ice offshore sufficiently to allow passage, or at least to make the risk of attempting it worthwhile. And, as Nikolai had predicted, it was on his birthday, that they passed successfully from the Kara Sea into the Laptev.

*　　　　*　　　　*

Ice as far as the eye could see! Now the voyage demanded a completely different type of sailing with the helmsman taking a careful course through the broken floes, as Ben records:

We reached the ice! Finally after twenty one days out of Murmansk, we've reached the pack ice. We can only go through thin ice because, despite the design of the boat, what limits our capacity to go through ice is how good the helmsman is at avoiding icebergs. So far we've done okay. When we got to the ice we had to take sails down and put the engine on so that we could manoeuvre properly. I really enjoy dodging in and out of the ice floes, it takes a lot of effort, you have to be aware of everything in front of you despite your restricted vision because boats don't turn very quickly.

Difficult enough in fine, calm weather but as the wind drops so fog silently blankets the surface of the sea making it almost impossible to discern what is water, what is ice and what is simply fog. Between the 9th and 14th August the crew play a game of hide and seek with the ice fields, taking a few steps forward as the seaway opens up only to be driven back as the ice closes in once again. This is especially frustrating as the Canadian ice charts now show the North West Passage completely free – if only they could get there.

Ben and Constance in particular are showing their metal as ace navigators through the ice and David reminds them that although it might be great fun, the ultimate success of the PoC may yet be scuppered if they venture too far into the ice which then closes in behind, trapping them. Watches now included anchor watch – making sure

BEN'S BLOG
4 August 2016

Given where we are I find it a great comfort to have a look at a map and see that a significant part of the journey is already completed. Indeed the part that we have already done has taken more time per nautical mile than any other point in the trip. After we cross the next passage we'll be steaming on ahead, no longer waiting for the ice to clear. After all the North West Passage is already open. The reason I do this is because I find action without gain really really depressing. I don't think there's anything I hate more than having put a lot of time and effort into a task and seeing that it is no nearer to completion than when I started.

BEN'S BLOG
11 August 2016 – Laptev Sea

When I woke up again I discovered that overnight the ice had moved and in the time I'd been sleeping we'd managed to leave the archipelago and were now heading southwards through relatively thin ice to the coast. When I came on watch we were merrily dodging in and out of the ice under sail with no swell and little cold. It was the most fun I've had in weeks.

Denis and David poling ice.

ice didn't accumulate around the anchor chain, and there was an additional risk of polar bears finding their way across the ice and on to the boat.

If caught in the open, a makeshift mooring was used to secure *Northabout* to a handy pan of floating ice – by no means ideal as by morning the vessel would be surrounded by ice requiring much huffing and puffing with poles to free *Northabout* from its grip. This free ice was also at the mercy of the wind and tide, moving at several knots and piling into other floes as it went. Much better to find a stamukha, a big lump of ice that had hit the bottom of the sea and become stuck, but even these can be unstable, as described by Ros in her blog of 12 August:

A stamukha is an iceberg that is touching the bottom. We had to turn round from the ice by the coast last night and find somewhere safe to moor. There were strong winds so we needed to find somewhere else to sit them out, and the answer was a stamukha. We knew it might drift, and it did, so when it had drifted into a more dangerous situation, Ben (who was on anchor watch) woke Nikolai and we've moved off it to go and have a look at the ice situation just up ahead again.

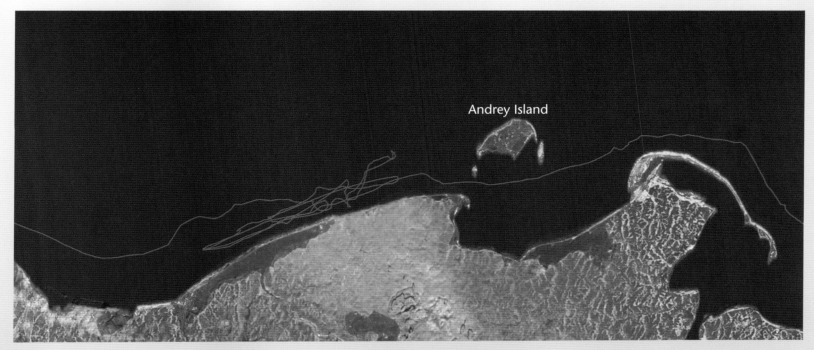

Andrey Island

This was a make or break time for the crew of *Northabout* and indeed for the success of the Polar Ocean Challenge. Every day lost in finding a path through the ice increased the likelihood of finding the ice closing in further on in the voyage. In that event, even if they found shelter on the mainland, overwintering would mean abandoning *Northabout*, with the crew finding their way home – in itself a monumental logistical nightmare. Almost unthinkable was a scenario where the vessel became entrapped in sea ice, far from shore, where rescue would be many times more difficult, and very costly.

A picture's worth a thousand words. This map shows the actual track of Northabout *from the 10th to 15th August showing the crew endlessly tacking backwards and forwards in order to find a passage through the ice. Eventually able to find a clear route through south of Andrey Island (Ostrov Andrei) they enter the Laptev Sea.*

The GoPro captures Northabout *being guided into the stamukha; Nikolai helming with Denis at the bow and Barbara emerging on deck.*

93

It was on these occasions that David and the crew could give thanks for the presence of Nikolai and Denis. Only a handful of sailors had the experience that Nikolai brought to the PoC, his knowledge of these waters and in sailing in ice provided huge reassurance to the others on board. During the trip Nikolai spoke of the last occasion on which he sailed through the North East Passage:

I've already done this route back in 1998–1999. My vessel Apostle Andrei and me were the first to do it in the history of yachting. Those years were very difficult in terms of the ice situation and therefore we had to spend a lot of time waiting for passages to open, and we even had to spend the winter in Tiksi because the trip could not be completed in one navigation season. Since then the ice situation has substantially eased, because of the climate warming the amount of ice has decreased and yacht sailing became almost problem free... and our hopes for this year were based on this relatively simple ice conditions, but unfortunately when we arrived here this year, to Laptev Sea specifically, it unexpectedly again got covered in ice and that hasn't happened in ten years, this kind of ice conditions, so the task ahead is not that simple.

Despite Nikolai's experience, in David's blog of 12 August, the frustration to-ing and fro-ing among the ice comes through clearly:

At present moored alongside a stamukha. Last night the ice started to converge and get thicker, so we slowly made our way closer to the shore, we even lifted the retractable keel, to get closer to the shore, but eventually the lead petered out. Our Island was in sight, with a large tall marker in the far distance. So close but so far. Having poured over the ice charts and Sat Photo, if only we could get to 111° East, our route would be free as far as Bristol. We wriggled around each patch of ice, backwards and forwards. Dennis was up the mast trying to find a route. It was too windy for the drone, and Ben was in bed. Slowly the ice all closed in. We must have tried every single option three times. Just 3 miles, but it could have been 300 miles.

The wind and sea state were really picking up. Our options were few. Wind and tide against us, really shallow water of 5m, small bergy bits in the water to miss. No shelter whatsoever. Do we make our way back the 40 miles where we knew a good anchor spot? At this rate it would take us 11 hours, using up precious diesel. In the end a nice large floe came into sight, so we gingerly approached, and my comrades made the boat secure. It would protect us from the sea state like a pontoon, and protect us from the mass of ice coming our way.

Perhaps to add to their problems, the weather forecast showed a severe storm heading their way with winds of 35 knots, gusting to 50. David's blog records the hours that followed:

The storm when it came was one of the worst I have ever experienced in Arctic waters. It doesn't matter where you are in the world, in a tent, or a boat, it can be scary to find yourself at the mercy of mother nature. Because Northabout *is so tall, she catches the wind and this, combined with the shallow water in which she was lying, where the waves are even more exaggerated, put tremendous strain on the anchor and chain. Thank God for Nikolai's experience. At the height of the storm he was with Denis helming towards the anchor, very slowly with the motor ticking over. I have never been taught this technique, or even read about it, but it saved the anchor.*

Meanwhile, I called everyone into the saloon for safety's sake and it was only after midnight that the winds started to abate. At times like this you think the worst. Does it build character? I'm sure it does, but I can think of easier ways to do it. One thing for sure, the team were great, and we will drink for years to come of that night. I gave Comrade Nikolai my vodka for the first toast – he'd certainly earned it.

Ben describes the events of the night of 12/13 August:

We had winds of around twenty-five knots when I went to bed. At some point during the night we all got up and went into the saloon because the wind was strong enough to be a bit of a worry. Denis and Nikolai went into the cockpit and steered the boat

Denis spotting ice from the mast.

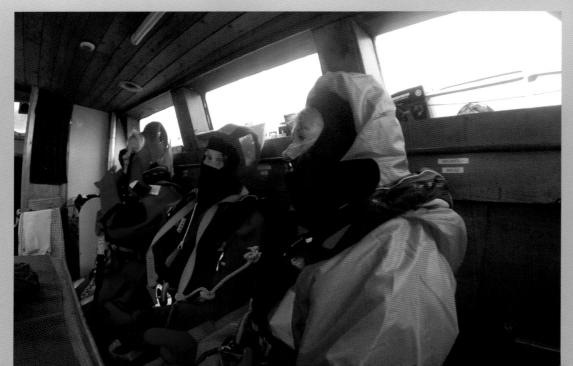

Ben captures his fellow crewmembers on the GoPro – Barbara, Ros and Constance in their survival suits waiting out the storm.

Sheltering from the storm behind Ostrov Severnyi on the night of 14 July.

LAPTEV SEA

Ostrov Severnyi

around so that at no point the anchor was being stressed. We had several hours of that before the wind calmed down again and we could go back to bed. In the morning we decided to leave to see if the ice had been moved out of the way by the strong winds. And it had. Over the next few hours we made our way along the ice until we came across a problem. A very shallow bit of water next to the coast was very nearly cut off by a large ice floe, the debate was whether we could get round it in the water. Nikolai put the keel up a little and we tried our luck, five minutes later he came back down and put it down again. So here we are, in open water, at last, we even have wind we're sailing along nicely.

Fortunately Nikolai knew of an island ahead that would provide shelter and it was here that they headed to wait out the worst of the weather.

*   *   *

It was eventually this storm that broke up the ice, pushing it away from the mainland out into the Laptev Sea. It had been a narrow squeak but a remarkable team effort to endure the frustration, the hard work, and the trials of close confinement while in the ice. Now *Northabout* was almost free of the shackles of the ice and the charts showed open water ahead, at least for the time being.

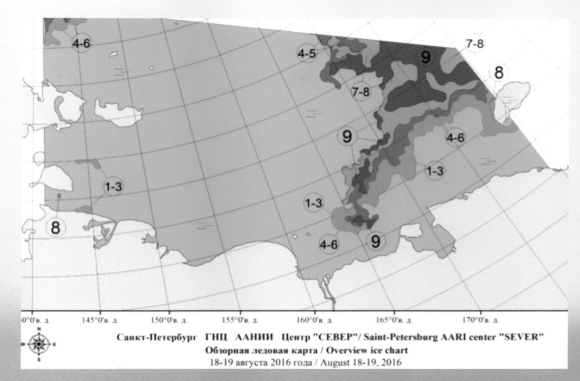

Санкт-Петербург ГНЦ ААНИИ Центр "СЕВЕР"/ Saint-Petersburg AARI center "SEVER"
Обзорная ледовая карта / Overview ice chart
18-19 августа 2016 года / August 18-19, 2016

Russian ice chart for 18-19 August showing the area of the East Siberian Sea. On the far left of the chart are the New Siberian Islands which guard the entrance, going west, to the Laptev Sea. On the far right is Wrangel Island, the approach to which is shielded by the remnants of the melting ice which means Northabout *taking a detour farther south to avoid it.*

Good progress is made over the following days and while there is a great deal of floating ice and bigger bergs to be avoided, the storm has clearly done its work in pushing the ice offshore. From here *Northabout*'s next waypoint is Wrangel Island on the far edge of the East Siberian Sea beyond which lies the Chukchi Sea and their destination, Point Barrow.

BEN'S BLOG
17 August 2016

Today in my morning watch things weren't quite as idyllic. Overnight we'd sailed into ice. I know, I said we shouldn't be troubled by ice for a bit, I was wrong. The ice on its own wasn't too bad, the thing was we had fog as well. The fog was terrible, we could barely see five metres in front of the prow and the ice just kept on coming. After a bit the fog went, thankfully, the ice didn't. Eight hours later when I'm back on watch we still had ice and even better, we had to divert to avoid a sandbank. Then the fog came back, typical. Luckily after another two and a half hours the ice began to clear a bit, for now.

Ben helming through ice and fog.

BEN'S BLOG
18 August 2016

We're still running into ice, aaaagggghhhh! We've had patches of clear water just large enough that you can't see the other side, just large enough that you start to think maybe we've seen the last of the ice, and then it looms out of the horizon like a piece of homework that you've been trying to avoid doing by moving to India only to find that school exists there as well. Hmpf. We've put in three new tracks today each one further south than the last in the vain hope that we'd finally escape the ice by running away from it. Unfortunately it seems that ice is a vindictive substance and refuses to leave us alone. Despite this we have still managed to head in a vaguely easterly direction and looking at a world map, it looks like the North East Passage is nearly done. From then on things will hopefully be more comfortable. Less ice, less distance to do than we'll already have done and so on. Okay, alright, I've just learnt that recently, very recently, ice has moved in from the north to the North West Passage, which means we've got lots more of it to look forward to.

Hopes of a trouble free passage to Wrangel Island are momentarily dashed when the engine starts playing up. 'Just as things were getting into a rhythm,' reports David, 'the engine starts over revving. We are so close but so far out here. Nikolai and Denis trying to solve the problem. If not, it is a slow sail from here to Alaska.' Fortunately the mechanical genius of the Russians once again come into its own and, with a thorough clean of the injectors and fuel lines, the engine is running sweetly once again.

The appearance of the sea and the sky appear to be taking on a different character as they sail east, with remarkable sunrises and sunsets and, at night, the wonderful presence of the aurora borealis. Constance records the closing of the day on 23 August:

Oh what a night!! Just when you might think we have seen it all, we have had another extraordinary display. The celestial bodies have come together to reveal an out-of-this-world spectacular. The sunset has given us an alpenglow, for hours on end, with the deepest of oranges, pinks and purples streaking across the sky. The sky is filled with friendly dragons, eel, fruit loops. A three-quarter moon has risen through the mackerel clouds, shining its light on a mirror of silver sea. It is so flat you could water ski, were it not for the bits of berg scattered about.

We are ice helming, by moonlight, in a fantasy land. It is a time of indescribable beauty. Laughing with delight, we pinch ourselves to be sure our eyes do not deceive us. And just when we though it could not get any better, the aurora borealis appeared, spinning in the form of a pinwheel across the sky, with Venus shining as its crown jewel. We are privileged to witness this magical kingdom.

Yet, not all the crew are quite so wonder-struck. Ben is finding the pressures of the month-long voyage bearing down on him, as he confides in his blog around this time:

I am miserable. A combination of lack of space, physical inaction and endless monotony means that at the moment I am hating every single second of the day. I thought I'd say this to help people understand that while physically this trip is incredibly easy, I at least am finding it very tough. The last time I saw anyone other than the six people on board with me was thirty-one days ago and I am frankly fed up with not being able to be on my own. I'm permanently restless because I am getting no exercise whatever and every single day is exactly the same. What really tops it off is that the end is by no means in sight. We're not even half way yet. Though I have enjoyed other parts of the trip I just wanted it on record that the North East Passage has not been a positive experience.

A perfectly understandable reaction in the light of things and perhaps a situation made more stark by being the youngest crew member by far. And indeed, two days later, following a number of supportive comments added by followers on the PoC website Ben's mood is lifted:

Though some of the comments were humorous and some were actually very helpful the reason they actually touched me is that I'm surprised that there are people out there who care about how I feel. Generally I just try to get on with things and not think about how I feel, so the fact that you actually took time out of your day to write those was a new and lovely experience. Thanks.

Constance at the helm, sunrise over the East Siberian Sea.

The aurora and moonlight.

It's 5000 miles since they left Bristol and on 24 August they sail past Wrangel Island at the entry into the Chukchi Sea. Here they cross the 180° Longitude, a major milestone standing on the other side of the world to Greenwich and marking the start of the journey home. Point Barrow lies 400 nautical miles to the west. All these significant points are all the more important to Ben, being the only crew member to have made the whole trip.

Yet for all the excitement on board, the Chukchi Sea, notorious for its wild weather and contrary winds, lives up to its reputation and makes for uncomfortable sailing, as Ben's blog of 25 August relates:

This is agony. We have less than sixty miles to go until we're half way round so of course everything seems to be going much, much slower. It's not though. We've got the genoa out for the first time in weeks and have been going along at over seven knots over the ground. The weather has been good, wind but not too cold, although, you remember that current that was supposed to help us through the East Siberian Sea? All and I mean ALL, of the experimental evidence that we've encountered supports the conclusion that it just doesn't exist. If it did we'd be going over eight knots, so I don't know what we're doing wrong but it's frustrating.

But the next day:

WHOOOOOOOOOOOOOOOOOOOOOOOOOOOOOOOOOOOOOOOOOOOOOO! We're done! We're done with the North East Passage! We're half the world away from home and we've finished the North East Passage! We've done it, we're the first British boat to have done this! We're doing eight knots over the ground, we'll reach Barrow tomorrowish and then we'll start on the North West and we're done! We're done! We're done we're done we're done we're done we're done we're done! I'll talk more later but the laptop's almost out of charge so I have to go, We're done! YAAAAAAAAAAAAAAAAY!

Ben in reflective mood composing his daily blog.

Ben on the morning before arriving at Point Barrow. Almost there and land can't come soon enough.

100

The North West Passage
The Third Leg of the Polar Ocean Challenge

CROSSING FROM RUSSIAN TERRITORIAL WATERS to those of the United States is, for Ben, significant as the rigours of the North East Passage, not least the time spent at sea on what is by far the lengthiest leg of the trip, played heavily him. But it's a relief felt by most members of the crew as crossing the Chukchi Sea had been particularly arduous, as Ros describes:

The Chukchi Sea is wild and we are wet, tired and hungry. We are into the second day of 25 to 30 knot winds, throwing the boat around and everything in it. Many people are feeling queasy and not managing to eat very much. We are being thrown around in the saloon whenever we try to do anything, such as make a cup of tea or cook dinner. I for one feel ill, weak (through not eating enough), and slightly sick all of the time. All of our kit is soaked from being washed over when we are on watch. We can't light the stove to dry things out or warm up because it doesn't work when we're heeled over. As Barbara put it, it's all she can do to get onto her watch. Her sleeping bag is soaked because the waves have been leaking through the forward hatch – so is Ben's, and Denis' whole bunk is wet. Nikolai has himself strapped into his bunk with bungees to sleep. David is not sleeping because his ley cloth is not keeping him in his bunk properly. Apart from that we are having a wild ride!

Point Barrow, or Nuvuk to the locals, is the northernmost point of the United States and also marks the limits between the Chukchi and the Beaufort Sea into which *Northabout* begins her voyage through the North West Passage.

BEN'S BLOG
26 August 2016

So, the news of the moment is we've completed the North East Passage. It's taken us forty days, lots of ice, five thousand two hundred miles, a polar bear, three unsuccessful fishing trips, three birthdays and two reworkings of the time but we have finally done it. We crossed the international date line yesterday, or technically this morning, just thirty six hours ago. Everyone was tired then so it wasn't celebrated which is a shame. We crossed it on my half hour on deck so I personally have sailed Northabout to the end of the North East Passage. Credit where it's due though – Nikolai and Denis, without them we all would have died five of six times now. According to the auto pilot we'll reach Point Barrow in the next eighteen hours, I can't wait, I might actually be able to set foot on land for the first time in what feels like years.

Shot by Ben on the GoPro camera, a sullen sea relfects the mood of the crew as they approach Point Barrow, Alaska.

THIRD LEG
Cape Barrow–Upernavik

POLAR OCEAN CHALLENGE

GREENLAND

BAFFIN BAY

CHUKCHI SEA

BEAUFORT SEA

Banks Is.

Davis Strait

UPERNAVIK

POINT BARROW

Baffin Is.

Victoria Is.

Tuktoyaktuk

ALASKA

CANADA

Having sailed from Murmansk on 21 July, Northabout arrives at Point Barrow on 28th August. The third leg of her voyage, through the North West Passage aims to finish at Upernavik in Greenland.

In the history of Arctic exploration Point Barrow has played a significant role. Explorers Frederick Beechey and John Franklin both failed to reach it, their ships becoming stuck in the ice. Beechey's men eventually reached it by ship's boat in 1826 and the following year Thomas Simpson walked to Point Barrow from his ice-bound vessel. Later expeditions used Point Barrow as a jumping off point for entering the far north.

For the crew of *Northabout* this was the changeover point – Ros and Denis leaving and Steve Edwards and Johan Petersen taking their berths. Johan, a Norwegian, has sailed the North West Passage previously and is to be navigator on this voyage.

STEVE EDWARDS' BLOG
27 August 2016

As Northabout approached Point Barrow, Ros and I could talk on mobile phones and they could see me flashing the headlights of the hire car to welcome them from a few miles out at sea – a poignant moment that I will always remember.

Barrow has a certain spartan charm typical of the world's remote outposts and its people are friendly, welcoming and brilliantly resourceful.

Here they were able to replenish food stocks and limited (hugely expensive) fuel suppies – this being collected from the local fuel station in plastic cans. Twenty-four hours later *Northabout* leaves harbour and heads into the Beaufort Sea for their next port of call, Tuktoyaktuk (Tuk), around 500 miles distant. But as if to thwart the new found enthusiasm among the crew, the sea gods immediately remind them of who is in charge. A strong and persistent headwind means constant tacking while a malfunction on the auto-helm adds insult to injury. Ben explains:

Joy of joys, the auto-helm's stopped working and we're back to helming by hand. This is a mixed blessing, on the one hand it's really irritating to have to helm in large swells and with a strong headwind because any movement you make is at first ignored, and then exaggerated by, the wind. So it's hard to keep a decent track and it makes it harder to look out for ice. On the other hand, moving and putting effort into the steering keeps you warm which is nice and it means you don't have to put as many clothes on which is also nice because when you go downstairs and it's twenty-four degrees it can get quite uncomfortable. I would rather have the auto-helm.

Luckily Steve's presence means they have their resident techie back on board and he diagnoses the problem as being fixable when they reach Tuk. With the charts showing no ice between Barrow and Tuk, Nikolai takes *Northabout* out to sea to avoid the worst of the weather, a tactic which fails as the headwinds continue unabated. While there remains a strong possibility of become ice bound as they progress through the North West Passage, there's some consolation, as David confides:

I keep it to myself but I'm relieved that from now on, if we do get ice bound, at least we'll be able to overwinter on either US or Canadian soil, making life so much easier from the standpoint of visas. Once in Canadian waters we are told to make daily contact with the Canadian customs people – who turned out to be extremely accommodating when it transpired Nikolai had the wrong visa.

Finally, on 1 September, they pass Demarcation Point marking the border between the USA and Canada, and as though this was some magical point of climatic separation, the wind drops and the sun bursts through on to a sparkling sea. That evening, as the sun sinks there is an impressive display of sun dogs and in the distance the mountains of Herschel Island appear as is floating above the horizon. The appearance of these phenomena, along with the magnificent aurora borealis and fata morgana, can never be predicted and for early adventurers in these water such visions represented fearful prophesies of disaster – while mirages and wild compass variations led to navigational errors that often had fateful consequences.

BEN'S BLOG
30 August - Beaufort Sea

Something that is very good though is the addition of a certain Norwegian to the boat. While Denis was nice and very good at the sailing we couldn't really talk to him and this made life a little, not much but a little, difficult. Johan on the other hand can speak very good English, is also a very good sailor and very nice to be around. He's got the attitude that I've come to associate with very tough, very confident people, with just a hint of silliness to their humour. It's a good combo. Apparently pictures of me washing up have become famous back home, on that matter I would like to set the record straight. Yes I have been washing up on my days but it's Constance Barbara and Denis that ruled the galley on the North East Passage. I don't think that's going to change, though Johan is a good cook.

Islands in the Sky

ARCTIC ATMOSPHERIC PHENOMENA: STORMS, SUN DOGS AND DIAMOND DUST

"I immediately, therefore, went on deck, and soon after it completely cleared for about ten minutes, and I distinctly saw the land, round the bottom of the bay, forming a connected chain of mountains with those which extended along the north and south sides. This land appeared to be at the distance of eight leagues; and Mr. Lewis, the master, and James Haig, leading man, being sent for, they took its bearings, which were inserted in the log... The mountains, which occupied the centre, in a north and south direction, were named Croker's Mountains, after the Secretary to the Admiralty."

Sir John Ross describes his infamous fictional 'Croker Mountains'; in fact a mirage, which in 1818 he reported as preventing him from proceeding west and discovering the ultimate gateway to the North West Passage.

Islands in the sky: the phenomenon known as fata morgana.

William Barentz was the first to record the phenomena of Sun Dogs on his voyage of 1596. "And when the sunne was about south south-east wee saw a strange sight in the element: for on each side of the sunne there was another sunne, and two raine bowes that past cleane through the three sunnes, and then two raine-bowes more, the one compassing round about the sunnes, and the other crosse through the great rundle; the great rundle standing with the vttermost point."

The moon also causes extraordinary effects. While conducting a funeral of one of his men he described the appearance of halos around the rising moon: "What a scene it was! I shall never forget it. The lonely Fox, almost buried in snow, completely isolated from the habitable world, her colours half-mast high, and bell mournfully tolling: our little procession slowly marching over the rough surface of the frozen deep, guided by lanterns and direction-posts, amid the dreary darkness of an Arctic winter – and all this heightened by one of those strange lunar phenomena, a complete halo encircling the moon, through which passed a horizontal band of pale light that encompassed the heavens; above the moon appeared the segments of two other halos, and there were also mock moons or paraselenae to the number of six. The misty atmosphere lent a very ghastly hue to this singular display, which lasted for rather more than an hour.

From *The Voyage of The Fox*, 1860.

A sketch by Fridtjof Nansen from his book The Farthest North (1895). "During the night we had an uncommonly strong aurora borealis ; wavy streamers were darting in rapid twists over the southern sky, their rays reaching to the zenith, and beyond it there was to be seen for a time a band in the form of a gorgeous corona, casting a reflection like moonshine across the ice. The sky had lit up its torch in honor of the new year – a fairy dance of darting streamers in the depth of night. I cannot help often thinking that this contrast might be taken as typical of the Northman's character and destiny. In the midst of this gloomy, silent nature, with all its numbing cold, we have all these shooting, glittering, quivering rays of light.

The first person to record the phenomena known as the Novaya Zemlya effect was Gerrit de Veer, a member of Willem Barentsz's ill-fated third expedition into the north polar region in 1596–1597. Trapped by the ice, the party was forced to stay for the winter in a makeshift lodge on the archipelago of Novaya Zemlya and endure the polar night. On January 24, 1597, De Veer and another crew member claimed to have seen the Sun appear above the horizon, two full weeks prior to its calculated return. They were met with disbelief by the rest of the crew and for centuries the account was the source of scepticism. The phenomenon was finally proven to be genuine being a polar mirage caused by high refraction of sunlight between atmospheric thermoclines. The Novaya Zemlya effect will give the impression that the sun is rising earlier than it actually should (astronomically speaking), and depending on the meteorological situation, the effect will present the Sun as a line or a square (which is sometimes referred to as the 'rectangular sun'), made up of flattened hourglass shapes as in the photograph.

A magnificent aurora borealis flickers above Northabout's *masthead* – one of many occasions when the crew were treated to such a display. Of course we now know how optical effects such as the aurora, sun dogs, halos, coronas and anticoronas, opitical haze and mirages occur. Likewise with Arctic meteorological phenomena including so called diamond dust and ice fog, but to early explorers these strange events gave rise to fear and superstition as occurred on the voyage of Captain Munck in 1619. 'They entered Hudson's Straits, crossed Hudson's Bay, and there, luckily finding a harbour, they were compelled to winter. The weather was very severe; the ice was nearly four hundred feet in thickness; brandy was frozen solid; and what the poor sailors judged to be frightful omens appeared in the sky – two suns, and an eclipse of the moon. Worse signs soon appeared – dysentery, scurvy, death. Out of the sixty-four men that formed the company of the two vessels, but two and the captain survived.'

A day after passing Demarcation Point the winds continue favourable and excitement among the crew comes through in their daily blogs. Ben who is enjoying having Johan and his father for company writes:

We get to Tuktoyaktak 'tomorrow'. I'm really looking forward to that. And we get to get off the boat, if there's a food place maybe have dinner off the boat and just walk around. Actually, interesting point, the Inuit towns are all dry. It's illegal to sell alcohol there but it's not illegal to buy it. The reason is that the Inuit have no resistance to the drug. It's never been around before so their physiology isn't able to cope, they get drunk and addicted very, very easily and it kills them if they have too much.

In the meantime we're hoping for aurora. During the North East Passage we had one night where there was an aurora that was worth seeing. Typically, almost everyone was asleep. Only Barbara and Denis saw it and since then I've been hoping the clouds will clear and it'll get dark earlier on my shift so that I can get to see some. No luck so far but I have a promise that if some are seen I'll be woken up.

While the western world looked with awe upon the courage of those early adventurers sent out to explore and open up the Arctic regions, the indigenous peoples of the region had less cause to celebrate. Along with a genetic intolerance to alcohol vast numbers of Inuit people succumbed to diseases brought in by the explorers – particularly Tuberculosis – which spread more readily as a result of giving up their traditional houses for warmer, more permanent, dwellings where living in closer proximity the disease was encouraged to spread.

Cultural changes were almost a destructive, as Fridtjof Nansen describes in his book *Eskimo Life* published in 1894. He bemoans the influence of Christian missionaries among the indigenous people of Greenland, writing of one such:

Father and son.

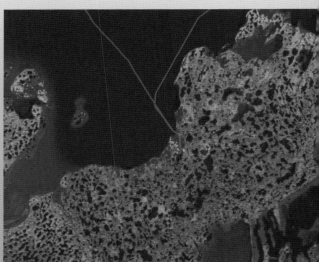

The tricky entrance to Tuk.

Evening and Ben get his first glimpse of Tuk.

107

Who complained bitterly of the difficulty of getting them to leave off the perpetual wanderings and settle down in one place so that he could preach Christianity to them at his ease: even proposed that they should be forcibly bound down to a less migratory life. If this pious man, who thought of nothing but the advancement of the Kingdom of God, had been living now, he might in so far have been happy; for the Christian converts of to-day scarcely travel at all. By reason of the great impoverishment which we have brought upon them, there are every day fewer and fewer hunters who can procure enough skins to make a woman-boat and a tent, both of which are of course necessary for travelling. They are more and more forced to pass the whole year round in the unwholesome winter houses, which are, of course, mere hot-beds for bacteria and all sorts of contagious diseases, while the men are thus unable to change their hunting-grounds, and must keep to the same spots year out year in. By this means the 'take' is of course greatly diminished, food is consequently much less plentiful, and the indispensable sealskins become fewer and fewer.

*　　　*　　　*

Throughout his time on *Northabout* Ben and his fellow crew members touch time and again on the importance of their sailing gear, on the miseries of not being able to find dry clothes – and on the pleasure of having the right gear for anything that nature could throw at them. Here in Tuk there was little evidence of the old way of life among the Inuit and even less evidence of their traditional dress. While hunting continues it is with rifles rather than harpoons, travelling in inflatables rather than kayak, or across the ice on skidoos.

There are churches representing a variety of religious various denominations in Tuk. This is the Anglican church.

The residents prefer modern textiles to the traditional sealskins.

With prohibitive fuel prices in Point Barrow it was decided to fill up while in Tuk, forgetting it was an extended holiday weekend. Fortunately the goodwill of the locals meant full tanks before heading off again. Here Barbara, Nikolai and David talk to the helpful tanker driver.

DRESSED TO KILL

"There's no such thing as bad weather, only bad clothes."

Norwegian saying

Ben and his family take their adventures seriously. Entering into such activities as the Polar Ocean Challenge is not to be taken lightly and such voyages offer up enough unforeseen difficulties without adding to them by under preparing. Along with food supplies, perhaps there is nothing so important as taking adequate and appropriate clothing on such a journey. While no novices on a sailing boat, Steve Edwards in particular being an experienced ocean sailor, the family recognised Arctic sailing required careful planning, and quality kit was essential. As Ben says:

The kind of gear a day sailor requires is much the same of the clothing sold for climbing and walking and we already had most of this from previous adventures. Heavy weather sailing gear is more specialist and I bought what I needed while we were on our various sailing courses in Suffolk. Cold weather sailing gear is more specialist still and while it's available online, I got what I needed on our stopover in Tromsø as with relatively cumbersome clothing it's always preferable to get a perfect fit.

Quality is one thing but quantity – on board a small vessel already crammed with crew and equipment – there is always a restriction on what it is prudent and practical to take. The two Russians, by far the most experienced in Arctic sailing, wore either impossibly lightweight clothing whenever the weather climbed above freezing, or donned Red Fox sailing gear, now Russia's leading supplier of such equipment.

Until recent times animal skins and furs were the only materials available to the peoples of the Arctic region for clothing.

Leaving Barrow in full cold weather sailing gear. Ben, Nikolai and Johan Petersen.

109

Waterproof footwear is one of the modern sailor's most indispensable articles but early explorers often found themselves seriously debilitated by ailments caused through continuously wet feet and by frostbite. Franklin's crew, equipped with the Royal Navy's standard leather sea boot, would have found that, while serviceable for most duties aboard ship, such heavy footwear was completely impractical for undertaking long treks across the ice as they later were compelled to do. In contrast, and using the most hi-tech materials available, the modern sea boot is a piece of superb engineering. Of the native people's traditional footwear, Fridtjof Nansen provides a detailed description in his 1894 book *Eskimo Life*:

On their feet they wear a peculiar sort of shoes, kamiks, made of seal-skin. These consist of two layers, an interior sock of skin with the fur turned inwards, and an exterior shoe of hairless, water-tight hide. In the sole, between the sock and the outer shoe, is placed a layer of straw or of bladder-sedge. Into these kamiks the naked foot is thrust.

A leather sea boot recovered from the remains of the Franklin expedition found at Starvation Bay. On the right is a modern Dunlop special cold weather boot of the type worn by Ben which includes a thermal lining and slip resistant soles.

For the Inuit peoples of the past, the resources they relied upon were almost entirely those which they found within the compass of their settlement. For personal warmth and protection in the harshest of environments the skins of larger mammals of the Arctic provided every item of clothing, and those early explorers of the Arctic region did well to adopt much of this native clothing for their own survival. Photographs of Nansen, Peary and others show them almost indistinguishable from their Inuit counterparts and these two explorers in particular adopted as much of the indigenous peoples' clothing as possible. Peary had clothing especially made for him and his team by Inuit women, declaring 'The traveller who goes upon the ice-cap without fur clothing does so either from ignorance or because he is reckless.'

The sea creatures from which the Inuit obtained both food and clothing were by no means easy prey. Seals, walrus, narwhal and whales presented great danger, not only because of their size and various armaments but also because the hunter had to enter their environment in order to capture them. As Fridtjof Nansen put it:

Traditional Inuit sealskin parka and polar-bear fur pants with sealskin waist.

Picture a people placed upon a coast so deserted and inhospitable as that of Greenland, cut off from the outer world, without iron, without firearms, without any resources except those provided by Nature upon the spot. These consist solely of stone, a little drift-wood, skins, and bone; but in order to obtain the latter they must first kill the animals from which to take them.

For this the hunter relied upon the kayak, a vessel which had been developed over centuries, reliant in its manufacture upon simplest materials readily available from which this fast, strong yet light, little craft was built. The hunter was held in highest regard among these remote communities, and little wonder for they put their lives on the line each time they ventured out to sea. In his book *Eskimo Life* Nansen describes a hunter at work:

Boas, one of the best hunters of the village, has seen a large he-seal far off, and has paddled towards it. There! a little way before him its round black head pops up. He bends well forward, while with noiseless and wary strokes he urges the kayak toward the seal. He quietly stows his paddle alongside, exchanging it for his harpoon. (1) Boas sits still and moves no muscle; but as soon as it turns its head away again, he shoots forward like a flash of lightning: the harpoon is seized and carried back over his shoulder, then with a strong movement, as if hurled from a steel spring, it rushes whistling from the throwing-stick, whirling the line behind it. (2) The seal gives a violent plunge but, quicker than thought, Boas has thrown the inflated seal skin bladder out of the kayak behind him which prevents the seal from staying underwater. When the seal resurfaces he paddles up to its side, and as it still moves a little, he gives it a finishing stab with his long-handled knife, pulling out his lances and replacing them in the kayak. He fastens the bladder to the seal and the animal is attached by means of the towing-line to one side of the kayak to be taken back to shore (3).

ern   methods: Greenlanders a seal, shot with a rifle and at the stern of their boat.

Home comforts. Ben and Johan enjoying a few hours in front of the TV.

On 2 September, six weeks after leaving Murmansk, Ben writes up his blog as *Northabout* slips into a sheltered harbour at the edge of the settlement of Tuk:

We're in Tuk! It's amazing! Forty percent of the land is small lakes and the village is built around it. It's bleak, like the rest of the Arctic, but there are some small hills and some foliage, so in comparison to the area around Barrow it's a veritable rainforest. We arrived several hours ago in an area away from the rest of the village because it's more sheltered and there's a hurricane in the US. When we arrived we refuelled and Nikolai and Barbara got a ride into town to see the pontoon near the village. They returned and proudly announced that they had procured not only the car they'd come back in, but also the use of a house for a shower! Not surprisingly we all went and had showers, it was very nice. We were also granted use of the television that it had.

While the rest of the crew took the opportunity ashore to get to know Tuk and to stock up with food at one of the town's two supermarkets, Steve was also able to track down an engineer, Willard Craig, and together they set about making a new spigot for the autopilot – a painstaking job requiring great precision to replicate the original part. Two days later, with these tasks complete and with no major signs of ice ahead, *Northabout* retraces her inward track and then heads east on her journey through the North West Passage.

DAVID HEMPLEMAN-ADAMS' BLOG
3 September 2016

It was blowing 35 knots and we were snug as a bug on a pontoon. Halyards slapping on the mast and lovely to hear from a warm sleeping bag. A great night after showers. To see the slick running down the plug hole was very satisfying. Then a huge work day. We all had our job lists, ice lights, bilge pumps, laundry, shopping but the man who gets the Vodka Salute is unquestionably Steve who with Willard fixed a broken pilot spigot. That sounds quite easy but it took the whole day in a machine shop in a container, working to fine tolerances, and then fitting it in the bowels of the lazerette in cold weather and driving rain. It worked first time. Brilliant effort. Tuk, what can I say. Famous from the 'Ice Truckers' TV series . Next year you will be able to drive from Near Cape Horn, in the Southern Ocean to Tuk, on the Arctic Ocean.

Tuk itself didn't have a lot to offer other than the warmth, hospitality and ingenuity of its people, including Willard Craig who, with Steve, engineered the new autopilot spigot.

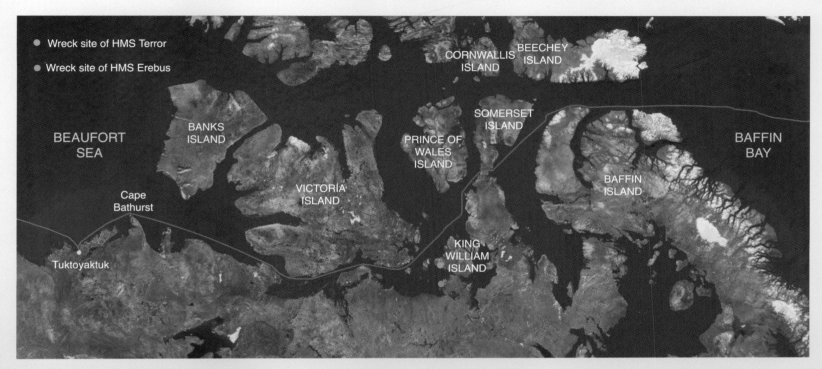

- Wreck site of HMS Terror
- Wreck site of HMS Erebus

BEAUFORT SEA

BANKS ISLAND

CORNWALLIS ISLAND

BEECHEY ISLAND

SOMERSET ISLAND

PRINCE OF WALES ISLAND

BAFFIN BAY

Cape Bathurst

VICTORIA ISLAND

BAFFIN ISLAND

Tuktoyaktuk

KING WILLIAM ISLAND

We left Tuk yesterday (Ben writes on 6 September). So far we've been very lucky, we've had following winds ever since we left and have been doing over seven knots most of the time. We're at one hundred and twenty six degrees at the moment, when we reach one hundred and twenty we'll be two thirds of the way round. Exciting prospect, we're almost done. In light of the lack of ice and in the spirit of saving time we've decided not to stop in Cambridge Bay or Pond Inlet and go straight on to Uper-navik in Greenland before doing our crew change. Looking at the ice maps at the moment it seems we'll be able to get through with little or no trouble, though this is almost bound to change, if it stays that way we'll reach Upernavik in about fourteen days. I'm looking forward to it!

Their original intention had been to take a short cut through the Prince of Wales Strait but the ice charts showed the passage was blocked and so Nikolai heads for the longer but ice-free route through the Amundsen Gulf across the foot of Victoria Island. These seas, with their multitude of islands, narrow straits and dead-end gulfs, are the grave-yards of many of the early would-be seekers of the North West Passage. Even today the route is fraught with danger but in times past, where winter ice completely blocked all possible passages, ships and their crews would be held fast for months, hoping their vessels would survive the crushing forces as the ice closed in.

Track of Northabout through the North West Passage starting from Tuk on 5 September and entering Baffin Bay on 13 September.

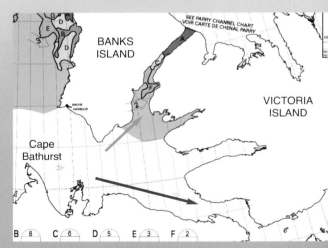

BANKS ISLAND

VICTORIA ISLAND

Cape Bathurst

Canadian ice chart. The red arrow points to the Prince of Wales Strait which is blocked by ice and so Northabout takes the ice-free pas-sage via the Amundsen Gulf (green arrow).

The track of Northabout between 6 and 9 September. Cambridge Bay represented the last possible overwintering site should the ice close in ahead and they would need to ensure that retreat to here was possible should the worst happen.

Even if their ship was freed as the summer came on, strange variations in the magnetic fields led these early mariners astray, while the maps of the region were, at best, often based on surmise. For Ben however, the likely success of his aim to complete both the North East and North West Passages in a single season seemed ever closer:

We're now in the North West Passage proper. We're further east than the outermost islands of the massive archipelago that is northern Canada. We are also two thirds of the way round the world. We reached one twenty degrees late yesterday night and are now in the last third of our trip. For the past couple of days we've had the most extraordinary luck with the wind, swell and current, they've all been behind us. I think we're doing an average of about seven and a half knots, continue like this and we'll be in Upernavik in eight days time. I really hope we continue like this.

Ben on early morning watch as Northabout sails towards Coronation Gulf. Fair winds and fine weather gave everyone hope that they would soon be through the North West Passage but as the temperature plummeted there was a real possibility of the ice fields ahead closing in.

Ben's wish comes true for on the 6th and 7th they continue to make good progress and push on through the Dolphin and Union Strait (named after the two small boats used by the naturalist John Richardson who explored here in 1864), towards Coronation Gulf.

On 8 September they passed Turnagain Point, named by Franklin as the furthest point east on his first overland expedition of 1819–21. It was while returning that the explorers suffered great hardship and starvation, surviving on lichen and ultimately eating their boots, after which Franklin became known throughout England as 'The man who ate his boots'.

But, as *Northabout* approaches Coronation Gulf, things began to turn against them, the wind coming head on making progress along Dease Strait and into Queen Maud Gulf painfully slow. This was very much their 'point of no return', but with Cambridge Bay receding over their stern it was vital that the ice charts continued to show open water all the way up to the Bellot Strait. Then, to add to their problems the magnetic compass begins to swing wildly, rendering it useless for navigation or at least confusing to the unwary. Many of the early adventurers to the region were caught out by the influence of the magnetic pole on their compass, leading them in the wrong direction, often into danger.

*   *   *

STEVE EDWARDS' BLOG
8 September 2016

As a young boy scout I was told to always trust my compass when navigating. That advice is good as long as you are in the UK, however in the North West Passage we are close to the magnetic North Pole and this has two effects. Firstly the North Pole magnetically is much closer than the real or 'true' North Pole, so we are going past it quite quickly and therefore the direction of apparent north is changing quite quickly. Secondly the earth's magnetic field is usually about horizontal and compasses are built assuming that this is the case. However when you are so close to the pole the magnetic field is mostly vertical as the field disappears into the ground to join up with the South Pole field in the centre of the earth. This means that not only are magnetic compasses quite unreliable in the NW Passage but that the errors can vary enormously from compass to compass depending on the details of how they are built.

Steve's photo showing the chart plotter at the time the magnetic influence of the pole was at its greatest. He points out in his blog that the symbol on the display which represents Northabout shows her heading is at variance with their true direction. 'This is because the navigation system is getting inaccurate information from its electronic compass which believes the boat is pointing at 105 degrees. The navigation system uses its GPS system to get both position and our real direction of travel so it is forced to assume that we have a very strong current pushing us sideways and is happy to accept pointing the boat is a very different direction from the course we are successfully following. The overall effect is that we follow the correct course as set out by the GPS but the boat symbol is pointing in a funny direction – all is well.'

L✸ST!

FINDING THE WAY IN ARCTIC SEAS

"Looking to the fact that little or no fresh food could have been obtained by the crews of the Erebus and Terror during their long imprisonment of twenty months, in so frightfully sterile a region as that in which the ships were abandoned, and also to the want of sustenance in spring at the mouth of the Back River, all the Arctic naval authorities with whom I have conversed coincide with M'Clintock and his associates in the belief that none of the missing navigators can be now living."

Francis M'Clintock on the fate of John Franklin, 1859

Sledge compass of the type used by British expeditions sent to look for Sir John Franklin between 1850 and 1853.

Following the shake down cruise to Svalbard and the consequential upgrading of much of the electrical and communications gear aboard *Northabout*, the crew were confident that navigation would not pose problems. The appointment of Nikolai Litau as skipper was further reassurance that, barring a major catastrophe, the voyage would be tracked precisely, both on board and by those watching the expedition's progress back in the UK.

No such surety was available for the earliest explorers venturing into the Arctic who were, we now understand, reliant upon the most primitive navigational aids such as the sunstone and lodestone compass. Those Norsemen who ventured west, settling in Greenland around AD980, also used the sun, moon and stars for approximate positioning, while their acute seamanship included the use of landmarks, tidal variations and even the movement of animals and birds to guide them.

Those who sailed into Arctic seas in the fifteenth and sixteenth centuries had a more purposeful reason for their adventures, paid by their governments and

'Summer on the Greenland Coast Circa Year 1000' by Jens Erik Carl Rasmussen (1841–1893).

commercial interests to seek the fabled North East and North West Passages that would open up faster trade routes between east and west. Armed with, among other devices, the magnetic compasses, the astrolabe, quadrant and backstaff, these mariners had means to establish their north-south position, although not until the introduction of the marine chronometer in the mid 1700s that accurate east-west positioning was possible.

Later mariners also became aware of the problems in using a magnetic compass as one approached the pole due to the variation between celestial north and magnetic north. By the late 1700s an instrument known as a dipping needle provided further help when navigating in northern regions whereby a magnetic needle pivoted to rotate in the vertical plane of the magnetic meridian with its rotation axis through its center of gravity so that it points in the direction of the earth's magnetic intensity.

Such anomalies made accurate map making a precarious occupation and reliance on early charts led many mariners astray, as did atmospheric phenomena of the sort which famously led Sir John Ross to 'discover' a complete mountain range that didn't exist.

As *Northabout* sailed past King William Island in the North West Passage, David muses on the perils of getting lost in these waters:

This is indeed a god-forsaken place if the elements turn against you, and one's thoughts turned again to Franklin and his crew held fast in the remorseless ice. It was about here, off King William Island in 1846, that Franklin abandoned his vessels and here, 170 years later, the remains of HMS Erebus *(in 2014) and HMS* Terror *(2016) were discovered by underwater archaeologists. Almost to the day, as we sailed close by King William Island, the world's press announced that the wreck of HMS* Terror *had been found lying in remarkable condition on the sea bed, her ship's bell being recovered and brought to the surface.*

Mercator's second draft of his map of the Arctic region 'Septentrionalium Terrarum' released in 1606. It depicts the North Pole as a large black rock, the Rupes Nigra, surrounded by a whirlpool into which four rivers flow. The rivers divide a continental land mass into four distinct regions.

Indeed no one who sails in these waters can fail to reflect on what has become the most enduring epic of Arctic endeavour: the failure of one man's attempt to conquer the North West Passage and the determination of those seeking to discover the truth behind the tragedy.

Pocket chronometer retrieved in 1859 from one of Franklin's boats abandoned at Erebus Bay on King William Island.

Ah, for just one time I would take the Northwest Passage
To find the hand of Franklin reaching for the Beaufort Sea;
Tracing one warm line through a land so wild and savage
And make a Northwest Passage to the sea.

Westward from the Davis Strait 'tis there 'twas said to lie
The sea route to the Orient for which so many died;
Seeking gold and glory, leaving weathered, broken bones
And a long-forgotten lonely cairn of stones...

folksong 'Northwest Passage' by Stan Rogers

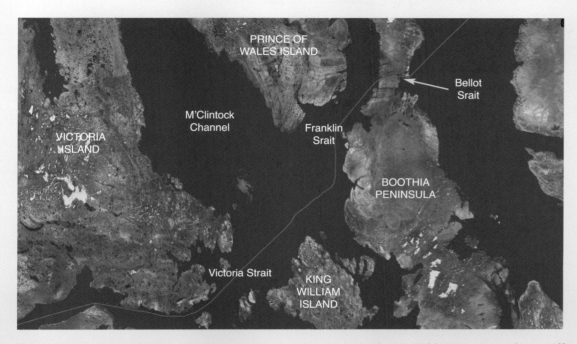

PRINCE OF WALES ISLAND

M'Clintock Channel

VICTORIA ISLAND

Franklin Srait

Bellot Srait

BOOTHIA PENINSULA

Victoria Strait

KING WILLIAM ISLAND

The track of Northabout *between 9th and 12th September. For a brief moment the crew have contact with the only vessel they've met in the North West Passage. This was the yacht* Polar Bound *belonging to David Scott Cowper, a legend in high latitude sailing, now bound for the Fury and Hecla Strait.*

BEN'S BLOG
9 September – Queen Maud Gulf

One word, grrrrrrrrr. I have damaged my ankle, any movement of it causes pain, and not the kind of pain that says you're doing the right thing it's just uncomfortable. Pain that says you're damaging it even more stop now you moron. I can still do my watches, but putting sails up and down and things are definitely out. To combat the swelling in my foot I've been getting buckets of sea water and putting my foot in them for two or three minutes. While this has had a huge effect on how stiff that foot has been the treatment has been more uncomfortable than wearing a wetsuit full of sand, trust me on that one!

Northabout was making good progress as they enter the Franklin Strait with a stiff breeze enabling both the mainsail and genoa sail to be set, although this presented problems for Steve Edwards at the helm:

The auto helm was having trouble stopping the boat turning into wind by about 40 degrees, but when it did the strange magnetic fields here meant that the electronic compass showed that the boat was actually rotating and this was shown on the chart plotter screen by the wheel. My first attempt at dealing with this, taking manual control, simply served to reinforce how hard even basic steering is in this environment. It was almost completely dark in fog with abut 100yds visibility so without a useful compass the only way I had of telling which way the boat was facing was the GPS course over the ground, which tends to be 10 seconds behind the reality and so not much use when you are being blown round by the wind and all the sail. I then realised that we would be better with much less sail and the genoa is both the easiest to get in short handed and the one which causes most of the trouble. Fortunately with this furled the boat became much easier to steer and when I had it pointing in the right direction and engaged the auto helm then all was well.

But at least there was (almost) no ice to make the situation truly dangerous and, indeed, it was not until through the narrow Bellot Strait that they spotted the first significant ice since leaving Barrow, as Ben's blog relates:

Steve taking in the scenery at the start of the Bellot Strait.

119

We're through the Bellot Strait! It's an almost completely straight passage between two islands lasting eighteen miles and cutting a huge section off the journey. It almost always has ice in it but as we went through today it was completely clear. It's odd, hundreds of people died trying to find the North West Passage. Caught by ice and storms they either froze or were shipwrecked. And we went through seeing a grand total of seven small floating ice chunks. If I hadn't already been through the North East Passage I might wonder what all the fuss was about. A grim testament to green-house gasses.

However, even a completely ice-free Bellot Strait did not disappoint and its transit was one of the highlights of the whole voyage for those who witnessed it:

As we approached, I think everyone was apprehensive. Everyone wanted to be on deck. The Bellot didn't disappoint. It is a deep sound that cuts through Boothia Penin-sula, providing a short cut to Somerset Island. The Southern shore of Bellot at Zenith Point is the northernmost point of the North American continent. and the strait was not actually transited until after the Second World War. We had zero wind, so the sur-face was like a mirror and the steep cliffs and hills looked just like Scotland. Raw

Johan surveying the awe-inspiring scenery as they enter Bellot Strait on 11 September.

beauty. We had worked out the best time for a transit from the tide tables, as there is quite a fast current. At one point we reached an impressive 11.9 Knots. You could see the swirls and eddies as we made our way down. It is only 18 miles long but we all stayed on deck. Transfixed by this special place.

Calm as the waters were not everything went so smoothly on deck. Determined to get a movie of *Northabout* as she sailed through the Strait, they decide to put up the drone. Ben takes up the story:

While we were in the strait we put the drone up. The Father was flying, he's much better than me so it seemed sensible. When he first took off things went wrong immediately. Because we were moving he had to get the drone away from the boat as quickly as possible. He didn't manage to and the drone collided with the windshield in front of the cockpit. The rotors smashed themselves to pieces and the drone upended itself on the deck. Not a good start. Very luckily none of the motors were damaged enough to stop it flying so we put some new rotor blades on and took it up. The Father managed to get it away from the boat this time. He got some really good footage and we managed to get it back on the boat safely. All in all, a success.

Steve deploys the drone.

Once through the Strait, *Northabout* enters the Gulf of Boothia and then heads north into the Prince Regent Strait between Somerset and Baffin Islands before entering Lancaster Sound. Here, at the tip of Baffin Island the ice charts reveal what they hoped would not happen – two bands of ice threatening to close off their passage into Lancaster Sound.

For David, this had the prospect of delivering the nightmare he'd hoped to avoid; the way ahead closed off to them and a long slog back to overwinter in Cambridge Bay. Only by the slimmest of margins, does *Northabout* slip through a narrow channel into Lancaster Sound there to be met by wall-to-wall ice floes, as Ben describes:

Ice! just when we thought it was all over. For the past day we've had the wind and tide behind us, we've been doing nine knots at times. So of course, right at the end of my watch we come into thickish ice just as it's getting dark. The next six hours were tricky. Weaving in and out, trying to find a route and occasionally gently nudging pieces out the way. We are now out of it again and moving swiftly on. But it seems the North West Passage wasn't giving up without a fight. I do however have a new candidate for scariest moment of the trip. It was the last half hour of my watch. We were going at nine point two knots over the ground and it was getting dark enough that helming was getting tricky. We'd seen some pieces of ice earlier and so were looking out and has the radar on screen. I was sitting on the plank at the back of the boat and saw a wave breaking about thirty meters off the bow. I then noticed that the white on the water wasn't going away, I grabbed the torch we keep up there and turned it on, there was a large piece of ice twenty-five meters off the bow that we were heading for at nine knots. I jumped down to the wheel, hit the standby button to disengage the auto helm and yanked the wheel sideways. The boat swerved quite wildly and we missed it by ten meters or so but I noticed I was now jumping at every breaking wave I could see. If we'd hit that we would've damaged the hull quite badly and I was distressed at how close it'd got before I'd noticed. I put the auto pilot back on and got David up. I explained the situation and said I thought we needed two people on deck. He agreed and soon enough we were seeing wave crests that turned into ice chunks and were using the torch. Barbara came up at that point and I went to bed, but I was a little worried I'd hear a nasty thunk and we'd have to get off in a hurry. This, happily, turned out not to be the case. The system devised a little later was one person would be at the helm and one at the bow with the torch. The helmsman would then see as the torch was swung around and do their best to not hit the ice. Luckily we can't see any more ice in front and there's a chance we're through all the ice.

The Canadian ice chart for 11 September showing the extent of ice on the entry into Lancaster Sound from Prince Regent Inlet en route for Baffin Bay. By hugging the coast *Northabout* is able to push, slip and wriggle through while, to the west, Resolute Bay and the Barrow Strait are already choked by encroaching ice.

Ice floes stand out starkly against the brooding coastline of Devon Island.

Northabout's track having passed through the Bellot Strait on 11th September, they then sail through the Lancaster Sound on 12th and into Baffin Bay, reaching Upernavik on 15th.

DEVON ISLAND

GREENLAND

Lancaster Sound

Upernavik

BAFFIN ISLAND

BAFFIN BAY

STEVE EDWARDS' BLOG
8 September 2016

Mountaineers and polar explorers still struggle a bit with protecting their faces from the extreme cold and biting winds in high mountains and polar regions. However the motorbike, quad bike and skidoo community have had this problem for years and have got it properly sorted out – the answer is neoprene face masks and they are cheap and work brilliantly in the worst conditions. I found this one in the car spares shop in Barrow being sold to locals for their quad bikes and skidoos. Benji used to watch the Transformers films, and I thought he would like the design. He is wearing it with Baffin Island in the background.

As the off-watch crew lay in their bunks that night their uneasy dreams were punctuated by the crunching of the ice hitting the side of *Northabout*. But once through Lancaster Sound, despite warnings of gales, on the 13 September, the weather clears and they enjoy a fine day's sailing despite the temperatures steadily dropping. Behind them, the current ice charts reveal huge amounts of ice filling Lancaster Sound – another close call! Writing up his blog for the day Ben lists some of the achievements on the voyage so far:

Reasons to be cheerful. Ben, David, Johan, Constance and Barbara pose for Steve as the crew near the end of the third leg.

POLAR OCEAN CHALLENGE

The trip isn't over yet but the difficult part is. While we aren't done with the trip yet it does put quite a few records to our names. Nikolai's the first skipper to do both passages twice, David and I are the first Brits to do both passages in one season and Constance and Barbara are the first women from their respective countries to do the same. Rather sadly however I just feel like we've simply crossed a line we drew on the chart plotter, which is of course exactly what we have done. It's not the end that really completes the voyage in my opinion. You don't really feel like you're done until you're in port.

Three days of storms crossing the northern part of Baffin Bay add to the frustration of feeling 'so near and yet so far' for Ben and the crew, and as *Northabout* heads slowly eastward she now enters that part of Baffin Bay down which huge bergs flow from Greenland's glaciers into the north Atlantic. These towering cliffs of ice present a new and different kind of hazard to the crew who thus far have survived various types of sea ice from pack ice to broken floes and stamukhas. Here for the first time they encounter large numbers of 'bergy bits' and 'growlers' – pieces of ice broken from glaciers and bergs – about the size of a half-submerged farm tractor, and just as dangerous to run into.

*   *   *

BEN'S BLOG
15 September

It's over! A total of ninety days, eight thousand and forty one miles and we are now the first British boat to have done the North West and East Passages in one season! Things have been difficult at times, seasickness, having to be tidy and a teenager, but it was without a doubt worth it. The Baffin Bay was horrid. Headwinds all the way and the worst swell we've had since the Chuckchi Sea. The last twelve hours have been steadily better. The swell slowly got smaller and I finally saw the Northern Lights, true they were kind of sad and pathetic but they counted. The last hour into Upernavik was amazing. Huge icebergs everywhere and islands in-between.

Sunrise catches the tip of a massive iceberg as Northabout *sails towards Upernavik, Greenland. Officially bergs are classified as having to be greater than 16 feet above sea level with a thickness of between 94 and 164 feet and must cover an area of at least 5382 square feet.*

Agonisingly close to landfall and with the capricious weather continuing, 15 September finds the crew enduring another day of slog across choppy seas in which Ben and two others suffer from sea sickness, Then, finally, towards the end of the day, *Northabout* edges her way into the harbour of Upernavik, an experience Ben records in his blog:

The last hour into Upernavik was amazing. Huge icebergs everywhere and islands in-between. Just before we tied up Johan fished a piece of ice out of the water for our celebratory coke/vodka (depends how old you are). This place is curious. A small settlement built on a slope on a smallish island with an airstrip above it. In the winter it's surrounded by ice and in the summer it's surrounded by icebergs. On that note, the North West Passage has already frozen behind us. So as it turns out we went through a very short window. The Victoria Strait closed almost as soon as we went through, the same was true of Barrow. So despite the very obvious melting that's been happening we were lucky to get through. The plan from here on in is fairly simple. We are now confident that we'll get home.

First view of Upernavik.

Alongside – after ten days at sea.

Greenland and Home
The Final Leg of the Polar Ocean Challenge

FOR BEN, ARRIVAL IN UPERNAVIK meant not only the completion of his record break-ing voyage through both North East and North West Passages, it also signalled the start of the final leg, the culmination of the Polar Ocean Challenge which only he – and *Northabout* herself – were to complete. Here he was also witness to the final crew change – yet another small challenge in adapting to working with a new team.

Those leaving are David, Johan, Barbara and Constance while Ros, Colin Walker, his wife Alison and Francis Gard join the crew for the trip down to Greenland's capital, Nuuk. Here, all will disembark except for Ben and Steve (who leaves in Quatorq, at Greenland's southern tip) who will be joined by the Atlantic crew charged with taking *Northabout* home.

But first there's the happiness of a family reunion, with Ros arriving to greet Steve and Ben. There's a brief but welcome chance to catch up on sleep ashore while the usual restocking of provisions is overseen by Ros (who has brought a home made lasagne with her from the UK – Ben's favourite meal!). Ben and Johan then refuel *Northabout*, siphoning from the canisters secured at the stern into the main tanks.

Dawn Upernavik: fishing boats and icebergs.

Family reunion: Steve, Ben and Ros.

BEN'S BLOG
16 September 2016

Upernavik is an odd place. It's a very small town built on a hillside. All the houses have half of themselves up on stilts so they're not leaned over. Because of the angle there aren't any normal streets, instead they've got winding roads that somehow manage to go past every house. The small harbour they have is inside a bay with a number of large and really quite impressive ice-bergs. There's no real pontoon for small boats.

Arrivals and departures. The crew who took Northabout *through the North West Passage pose aboard while in Upernavik. From left: Ben Edwards, Steve Edwards, Johan Petersen, Constance Difede, Barbara Fitzpatrick, David Hempleman-Adams and Nikolai Litau. Above: David leaves for home in typical swashbuckling style.*

STEVE EDWARDS' BLOG
19 September 2016

The icebergs were between the size of telly to the size of a house to the size of a grand hotel. Even as we watched they were breaking up, creating lots of small bergs and ice chunks that lie on or just below the surface making them difficult to spot, especially with a large 10 foot swell, and suddenly appearing and disappearing in the water around us. Another danger with icebergs if you get too close to them is that they can invert, i.e. turn over in the water. We passed a couple that looked like they had already done this and had their 'bottoms' up to us.

There's also a poignant moment saying farewell to the Expedition leader, David, who manages to add levity to the moment of leaving *Northabout* by pushing his wordly goods along in a supermarket trolley

Two days later, on 19 September, they arrive in Ilulissat having endured some foul weather and seasickness among the crew. Ben describes some hairy moments avoiding a sea littered with icebergs:

We had a lot of icebergs in the dark and high winds, so we decided to have three people on watch, one on the helm, one at the front of the boat with a powerful torch and look out for ice and then one in the saloon at any one time warming up. By the time I was on watch it was light again so we could dispense with the torch man and have two people on watch again. A couple of hours later we tied up in Ilulissat. The approach was littered with icebergs and we had to go close to the coast to get in. The density of icebergs bizarrely is because of increased melting in the glaciers, they are not sea ice. The glacier is melting faster so more bits are breaking off and clogging the surrounding area so the more icebergs the warmer it is, or rather vice versa. We are really

Above: Alison and Colin Walker with Steve en route to Iliussat.

Left: Ben, Ros and Steve at the Icefjord.

lucky to have sailed into Ilulissat. With the Passages over and a fresh crew this really feels like a holiday now. Despite the high seas and sickies we're all having fun and the rest is greatly appreciated.

It's clear that Ben's enjoyment of Greenland was not just based on relief at finishing the major part of the PoC for he has since returned to Greenland on *Northabout* and has every intention of returning again. His mother Ros described it as 'a magical place' and, indeed, its dramatic scenery, its remoteness and its place in history, folklore and legend cloak Greenland in mystery. Certainly this part of the trip was a highlight for Ben, a sentiment shared by Ros:

Well what a completely awe-inspiring and joyous few days back on Northabout *to sail down the coast of Greenland. While in Ilulissat we walked up to the Icefjord – a spectacular jumble of ice fed by the large glacier. This had been recommended to me by a seasoned high latitude skipper who said that he has seen a lot of ice but this is quite something. Greenland is trying to develop its tourist industry and with sights like this it certainly has something to sell. Actually I like Greenland very much – lovely jolly, often funny, people and breathtaking scenery. I plan to come back and do some walking or ski trips here.*

GRØNLAND

ERIK THE RED AND THE VIKING LEGACY

Erik and his people were outlawed... he sailed oceanwards under Snæfellsjokull, and arrived at the glacier called Blaserkr. The following spring he proceeded to Eiriksfjordr, and fixed his abode there.

From the 'Saga of the Greenlanders'

The *Saga of the Greenlanders* relates how in AD982 Erik the Red, having been declared an outlaw in his homeland, decided to sail for a land sited by his fellow countryman Gunnbjorn when blown off course during a storm. Finding the western side of Greenland not unlike his homeland, here Erik founded a settlement in Erikfjord, now called Tunulliarfik Fjord, close to Qaqortoq, one of *Northabout*'s stopover ports. Later, returning to Iceland, Erik set about persuading others to join him. To encourage this, it is said, he painted a glowing picture of his new domain, a land with rolling pastures – the place he called Greenland. Leading 25 ships with would-be settlers, of which only 14 vessels survived the voyage, three settlements were eventually established and archaeologists today have identified over 500 individual farms from this period.

Recent archaeological discoveries suggest that these early settlers may also have been encouraged by the establishment of a lucrative trade in walrus ivory, highly prized in Europe,while the Inuit traditions of carved shamanistic figurines, called Tupilaq, may well have been instrumental in the foundation of such trade.

There are suggestions that the climate had been warmer at that time. Today scientists are predicting the possibility of an almost ice free Greenland within a century. The rapidly melting ice sheet, which contains water equivalent to a 7.4 metre rise in global sea-levels, is evidenced by the greatly increase calving of icebergs from glaciers such as those seen by Ben on his visit to Ilulissat. Due to these changes Greenland is set to become a major tourist destination – perhaps fulfilling Erik's original dream of a bountiful as well as a beautiful land.

A Tupilaq figure carved from walrus ivory. The trade in ivory from the creatures of the Arctic is thought to have existed from the time of Erik the Red and reached its height in the nineteenth century. Elizabeth I is said to have paid £1000 for a narwhal tusk such was its rarity.

Contrary to popular belief Viking warrior helmets were not adorned with horns.

ROS EDWARDS' BLOG
20 September 2016

The coast of Greenland is fed with icebergs from calving glaciers. We spoke to a trawlerman who said that over the last 20 years he has seen the ice problem move from the winter to the summer – they don't really get sea ice any more, the sea is too warm for it to form in any quantity, but they have a serious ice problem in the summer from the icebergs which are a result of an increased rate of glacier calving because summer temperatures are higher.

View over the Icefjord showing icebergs calving from melting glaciers.

Reaching Upernavik on 16 September North-about sailed southwards down the coast of Greenland where various crew members left or joined the boat. On 3 October they depart Prins Christianssund for the Atlantic crossing, arriving in Westport on 13 October and returning to Bristol a week later.

GREENLAND

1 Faeringehavn
2 Qaqortoq
3 Fiskanaesset
4 Prins Christianssund

BAFFIN BAY Upernavik

Illulissat

ICELAND

Nuuk
1
2
3
4

FINAL LEG
Upernavik – Bristol

POLAR OCEAN
CHALLENGE

Westport
Dingle Bristol

ATLANTIC
OCEAN

No pushover. Nikolai could be tough but his experience helped make his crew into confident sailors.

Photographer and film maker Frances Gard who joined Northabout in Upernavik for the voyage to Nuuk. Frances had helped David Hempleman-Adams in the early planning stages of PoC.

Ben had also by this time more than proved himself as a sailor (ironic that he'd been judged too young to receive the Day Skipper Course certificate), and taken to be no less a helmsman than any other of the crew. Indeed he and Constance were considered to be masters of sailing in ice – no mean accolade with Nikolai as your Skipper. And as David later said of him: 'I was very pleased that my judgement in asking Ben along on the PoC was fully justified. Ben began the voyage as a boy and returned a man.'

*   *   *

Having left Ilulissat heading for Nuuk, the voyagers continued to be entertained by the size and variety of icebergs they were now sailing among. On 21 September they once again cross the Arctic Circle and that night they are treated to a truly awe-inspiring display of the aurora – as though the Arctic was providing a spectacle of farewell to *Northabout* and her crew. The next day Ros records in her blog:

Frances is a tiny, slim, bright-eyed enthusiastic and clever lady who is always cheerful, and I suspect her of having a touch of magic about her. She came onto watch at 2200

BEN'S BLOG
21 September 2016

We've crossed the Arctic Circle! For the first time in months I am no longer in the land of the midnight sun. Naturally though we still have Northern Lights. Over the past two nights the aurora have been really spectacular. The night before last we had a circle of them directly above the boat and last night there was a green line in the sky almost exactly above where the circle is.

and around 2220 we started to spot signs of a building aurora – lightening sky with streaks up into space. By 2330 we got the rest of the crew up. Almost all of the sky was full of streaks and ribbons. We were encased by a cone of streak of light that met in a dancing, glowing point a long, long way above the mast. The light was mostly green but for a time we had green and red light swirling round at the apex of the cone. Undulating ribbons of light were closer to the horizon. Ben said it was very nice but was tired (he has done a couple of extended watches while the new crew were feeling sea sick) and went back to bed. The rest of us (Frances, Steve, Colin, Alison and me) crammed into the cockpit, glued to the spectacle above us – even Nikolai, who has seen some spectacular aurora in his time, kept popping up to have a look

In many ways their arrival in Nuuk marked something of a crossroads in the whole voyage. The departure of Nikolai signalled the end of the 'Polar' element of the 'Challenge' and while there was yet some hard sailing to be done there was a sense that this leg was in itself a different kind of adventure. Ben described the arrival of the Atlantic crew in his 23 September blog:

So, yesterday morning we pulled into Nuuk and were met on the dock by our new Skipper, Mike Stewart. Mike quickly established himself in my mind as serious about the job and pleasingly understanding about my worries about being on my own in a boat with four strangers. Not long after his first mate Andrew Coulthurst turned up, Andrew also seems to be serious and capable on a boat. That evening we met the rest of the new crew, Rob Hudson and David Wynne Davies.

A kind of crossroads. The signpost at Nuuk airport.

133

POLAR OCEAN CHALLENGE

Looking across the stern of Eagle's Quest II into the harbour at Nuuk.

Of the crew from Upernavik, only Ben and Steve remain, with Steve due to depart before *Northabout* begins her Atlantic crossing. Meanwhile Nuuk provides another opportunity for restocking and refuelling and, for Ben, a chance to record some more video interviews for the Wicked Weather Watch website and to meet the local inhabitants including fishermen and a reindeer hunter. Sharing a nearby pontoon was a yacht they'd met earlier, *Eagle's Quest II*, something of a luxury vessel compared to *Northabout*'s more workaday appearance.

On 24 September *Northabout* leaves Nuuk heading first for the small anchorage at Tunulliatsaap Nunaa, then on to Faeringehavn, Qarqutoq (where Steve leaves the boat), Fiskanaesset and Prins Christianssund from where the Atlantic crossing will begin. David Wynne Davies contributes his first blog:

Slipping out of Nuuk on a cloudy morning we instantly came across our first iceberg. It was relatively small but majestic with turquoise colouring below the waterline. Our track took us South for 30nm to an anchorage close to a deserted clutch of buildings. The following morning using motor we set off 60nm to Fiskenaesset, a small fishing community of perhaps 100 houses where we met up again with Eagle's Quest II.

BEN'S BLOG
24 September 2016

My first day with the new crew. I loved it! I woke up at about half eight. Dad had gone up to the hostel to send the video from the interviews so I stayed in the boat and helped David and Rob with the jobs we needed to do. We emptied the lazaratte so we could check the autohelm repair Dad and I had done in Tuktoyuktuk and after that we checked the sails and went though all the basic boat checks you have to do. At one o'clock we said farewell to Eagle's Quest *and left the dock. We'd agreed with them where we were going to anchor and we gave them our route so they could come and meet us. The sailing was beautiful, flat seas, no wind which was unfortunate, but the views made up for it. We only went about thirty miles but found a really nice anchorage with an old abandoned hamlet nearby.*

On 26 September, anchored near Cape Desolation at the south-western tip of Greenland, new crew member Rob Hudson records his thoughts:

After last night's northern lights spectacular I woke this morning in this cold remote anchorage to the sunrise and flat calm water. We feasted on porridge, and then Steve flew the drone to capture the moment, and we upped anchor aiming for Julianehavn late this afternoon. We soon saw ice, but little need to take avoiding action. I stood at the bow for a while and a whale was seen blowing a couple of times in the distance. The planned inland route was abandoned as the passage looked too shallow, so we have gone offshore.

Steve, Andy Coulthurst, Rob Hudson and Ben step ashore from the dinghy in Fiskanaesset where Ben discovers reindeer remains at the back of the harbour.

A spectacular drone's view of Northabout *at anchor*

135

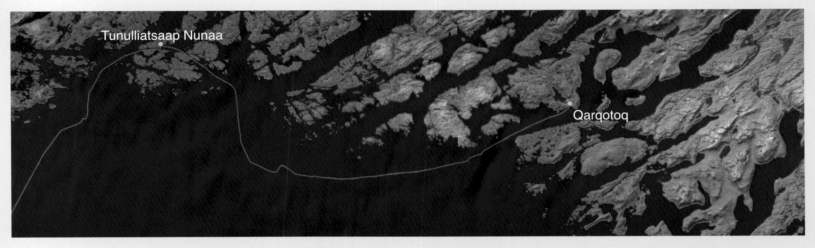

Tunulliatsaap Nunaa

Qarqotoq

From the shelter of the natural harbour at Tunulliatsaap Nunaa, on 28 September Northabout *arrives in Qarqotoq from where Steve is to leave for home.*

After days of fine weather and amid the wonderful scenery of Greenland's scattered islands, *Northabout* sails into the harbour at Qarqotoc where Steve is to disembark. On 1 October David Wynne Davies continues his blog:

The next leg involved a night passage South past Cape Desolution to an almost land-locked bay opposite Pinguiarnneq Island. It had been a long haul of about 180nm under brilliantly clear skies – memorable for the fantastic display by the Northern Lights and the sighting of several pods of humpback whales. One breached only 50m off our port beam.

These waters were once one of the richest whaling grounds, bringing whaling ships in their hundreds from Europe and North America. These vessels, and the men that crewed them, were the precursors of all those who followed in order to exploit the riches of the Arctic seas.

Qarqotoq, formerly Julianehavn.

A humpback whale breaching.

136

Plunder!

ARCTIC EXPLORATION AND EXPLOITATION

"A couple of hours after my watch I was called up to witness whales jumping out of the water and crashing back down in a huge splash. I've never seen anything like that before. Something that heavy managing to push itself ten to fifteen feet out of the water on a tail. Astonishing!"

Ben's blog 27.9.16, rounding Cape Desolation.

137

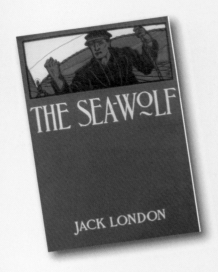

Commercial sealers killed the animals in their thousands, usually landing from the main ship in smaller boats among the 'rookeries' where they would wade among the packed seals clubbing them to death. Shooting was frowned on as this might ruin the pelts, with the skin of young fur seals being particularly prized.

Inuit hunters killing a walrus. Note the early use of a musket on the left.

"Why, if there is anything in supply and demand, life is the cheapest thing in the world. There is only so much water, so much earth, so much air; but the life that is demanding to be born is limitless. Nature is a spendthrift."

From *The Sea-Wolf* by Jack London

The quote above embodies the view of those times that nature was indeed in limitless supply. Today we know different. The natural world as we know it is under threat – and nowhere is this more starkly illustrated than in the polar regions of the planet.

Seal and walrus hunting

Jack London's dark adventure story, *The Sea Wolf*, set aboard a seal-hunting schooner at the end of the nineteenth century, provides the reader a vivid description of the harsh conditions endured by the crew of vessels such as the *Ghost*. While the indigenous peoples of the Arctic have been hunting seals since prehistoric times, European interest began in the sixteenth century when the first seal skins were brought back by itinerant mariners.

Seal hunting, along with the slaughter of other large pelagic animals, developed in earnest from the early 1700s, with the demand for oil, meat and skins resulting in the development of hunting on an industrial scale. Newfoundland was a principal base for a schooner fleet of some 300 vessels which by the 1830s was bringing in around half a million carcasses annually. Eventually purpose-built steamships with greater range

On their return to Greenland in August 2017 Ben and his family accompany an Inuit hunter from the small settlement of Siorapaluk on the western coast, north of Baffin Bay. Though not endangered through hunting, seal populations are under threat through the rapidity of melting Arctic ice. Drifting ice acts as a vital refuge for a mother seal with a pup, not only as a safe haven from predators but as a place for the pup to rest. Without these drifting rafts of ice on which to rest many pups will drown through fatigue.

and storage capacity took over from the smaller boats and for much of the rest of the nineteenth century these maintained a catch of close to 400 000 seals annually, devastating the seal population in Arctic waters.

Controls through the establishment of treaties and conventions began as early as the 1890s but it was not until the 1960s and '70s that meaningful protection was put in place. Traditional Inuit methods of hunting had little effect on the seal population, hunting as they did almost exclusively for subsistence and taking only what they needed from the plentiful stocks available using methods described elsewhere in this book. The introduction of the rifle and mechanised transport changed this but the overall demand for seal products has prevented over-exploitation. Today only a handful of nations, Canada, Greenland, Namibia, Norway, and Russia continue to hunt seals, while the USA enforces a complete ban except for its indigenous peoples whose operations are controlled by quotas.

Ben (left) watches as a Narwhal is dragged ashore at Siorapaluk (the most northerly civilian settlement in the world) having been shot at sea. Inuit are allowed to hunt this whale species legally for subsistence. They prize the animal for its large quantities of fat and almost every part of the narwhal, meat, skin, blubber and organs is consumed. The skin is an important source of vitamin C which is otherwise difficult to obtain.

'Dutch Whalers near Spitsbergen' painted by Abraham Storck in 1690 depicts a wild scene of hunters killing walrus, polar bears and whales and taking their carcases back to half a dozen whaling ships moored among the ice floes of the islands.

"As for me, I am tormented with an everlasting itch for things remote. I love to sail forbidden seas, and land on barbarous coasts."

From *Moby-Dick* or, *The Whale*, Herman Melville

Whaling

It was in hunting the whale that much of the earliest exploration of the northern polar regions came about. Small fortunes were to be made by those who owned the vessels that struck out on voyages sometimes lasting for upwards of two years and many such ventures came to grief when vessels became ice bound.

Whalers began hunting whales in the Arctic as far back as the sixteenth century. By the eighteenth century, many European ports were sending fleets of whalers to Greenland and the Davis Strait, and in the 1800s a large population of bowhead whales was discovered in the Bering Sea. American ships sailed north from ports such as San Francisco, and a new assault on the whales began, heralding in the great age of whaling as Melville describes in *Moby Dick*, published in 1851.

The season was short with whaling ships entering the Arctic as soon as the ice had melted enough to permit passage, and only the foolhardy or the desperate lingered past late summer. Many ships were lost as ice closed in around them.

By the late 1800s, a number of whaleships, those constructed to withstand the crushing force of the ice, were wintering in the Arctic. For these, it was not the ice that was to be feared but the perils of fire breaking out on board, as Captain John A. Cook describes in his 1857 memoir of whaling *Thar She Blows!*

Now of all the perils that threaten Arctic voyagers that of fire is the most dreaded. It is feared more than ship crushing. A ship may be caught and crushed to the sinking point between floes and yet remain above water for hours, or days, upheld by ice pressure, allowing ample time for the provisioning of boats preliminary to striking out across the ice-locked ocean desert for the distant, frozen land. But when an ice-locked ship becomes fire-smitten far from shore, God help the crew! Little opportunity to adequately equip for the long cross-sea flight is then afforded, the fierce heat quickly driving the men, practically empty handed, to the ice overside to escape shriveling, while the highly combustible nature of the cargo and the oilsoaked condition of the ship itself insures their swift dissolution.

A scrimshaw. Whalers carved scenes on whale teeth, walrus and narwhal tusks to while away the hours on board, bringing these exotic keepsakes home for family and sweethearts.

The impetus that drove these ships and their crews to venture into such dangerous waters was the demand for whale oil. Before the discovery of petroleum, this commodity was used as fuel, to make soap, and literally to lubricate the machinery of the Industrial Revolution.

Baleen whales, including right whales, blue whales and humpbacks, were prized also for the elastic, horn-like material forming fringed plates hanging from their upper jaws and used to strain plankton from the water. Before the invention of plastics, this flexible and incredibly strong 'whalebone' was used to make parasol frames, whips, fishing rods, corsets and hoop skirts. Then fashioned changed, and with mineral oil becoming abundant, the whaling industry rapidly declined in the early years of the twentieth century and whales species increased in number.

Today the threat to the seas and creatures dependent upon the oceans come from different sources – almost certainly more deadly than anything that has gone before and most of it the result of the influence of man.

Global Warming

As Ben and his companions proved, what was once a region made impenetrable by ice has rapidly become open water, ripe for exploitation by the military, by mining and by tourism. Already commercial shipping and cruise liners are regularly sailing through the fabled North East and North West Passages in almost ice-free waters. In 2018 the Chinese announced the intention of opening up a maritime 'Silk Road' bringing goods to the west via the Arctic. Periodic melting of the ice is not a new phenomenon – in 1660, on hearing of ice free conditions, Daniel Melgueiro made the North East Passage from Japan. We also know that the years immediately preceding 1660 were the warmest in over two centuries and such warming events are by no means unique. There are those that argue the current ice melt is but another such cyclical event – though science weighs against that view.

Certainly the nineteenth century scramble to 'discover' these northern sea routes was in part kicked off by reports between the years 1815-17, of remarkable changes in the Arctic oceans – as recorded in the 1817 minutes of the Royal Society:

"It will without doubt have come to your Lordship's knowledge that a considerable change of climate, inexplicable at present to us, must have taken place in the Circumpolar Regions, by which the severity of the cold that has for centuries past enclosed the seas in the high northern latitudes in an impenetrable barrier of ice has been during the last two years, greatly abated..."

Scientists recently described the current rapidity of change as 'the new normal' for the Arctic, citing air temperature rises of 1.6°C above the average, with sea ice decline being the greatest ever recorded and sea temperatures in the Barents and Cukchi seas 4°C above average, rising half a degree centigrade per decade since 1982.

The full consequences of these changes have yet to be determined but the resultant increase in ocean algae blooms contributes to accelerated sea temperature rises and

A painting by Thomas Binks of the whaling ship Dauntless, *which was caught in ice and sank off Greenland in 1829. Here the crew can be seen salvaging the ship's contents and creating a temporary shelter on the ice.*

The Arctic's iconic creature is under threat. The use of tracking collars reveals that bears are having to travel greater distances to find food while the reduction in sea ice means it's harder for them to catch prey.

In 2017 a Russian tanker made the transit of the North East Passage from Norway to Korea without an icebreaker escort, for the first time.

Greenland. Northabout lies offshore while the crew examine depressing piles of plastic and other rubbish lying on the beach.

Cruise ship off the coast of Svalbard. This is a relatively small vessel but, as the seaways become clear of ice, ships carrying thousands of passengers will become common. The vessel Crystal Serenity, carrying 1700 passengers, was the first large cruise ship ever to navigate the North West Passage, in August 2016.

warmer air encourages plant and alga growth on land, particularly affecting landscapes such as Greenland's where dark patches of growth on the ice means greater absorption of sunlight. Overall, the melting Greenland Ice Sheet, a major contributor to sea-level rise, continues to lose mass, as it has since 2002 when measurements began. On the North American continent sea level rises have washed away traditional Arctic settlements resulting in some of the first 'climate refugees'.

While climate change activists point to manmade hazards such as greenhouse gases, powerful lobbies reject the changes as other than natural. But whichever side of the debate one stands, the actuality spells desperate times for the wildlife and the indigenous peoples of the Arctic.

Human Encroachment

Almost as great a threat to the environmental changes in the Arctic will be the inevitable invasion of the region by those seeking to exploit both its rich mineral resources but also to 'mine' the region's exceptional landscape, attracting tourism of every kind.

Russia, with an eye on protecting its northern boundaries, along with the potential wealth to be extracted from the Arctic's natural resources, had been expanding its already significant military presence in the area – with consequent effects on the environment. They are not alone among nations wishing to secure interests here while all resist the idea their presence will be damaging.

It is yet to be fully understood what the impact of greatly increased tourism will mean for the region. Companies promoting their excursions often do so on the basis of a chance to witness a pristine environment, largely untouched by human presence. But cruise ships carrying thousands of individuals will require onshore facilities to service their vessels, handle waste, and provide entertainment for their clients.

The world has more recently woken up to the dumping a plastics into our oceans and its effects on wildlife and the environment. Perhaps in the long term our overuse of plastics will ultimately be the greatest peril of all.

Ben's crewmates on the Atlantic crossing, from left: David Wynne Davies, Andrew Coulthurst, Mike Stewart (Skipper) and Rob Hudson.

Sunset on Geenland.

At the southernmost tip of Greenland lies Cape Farewell, aptly named, for southwards lies the open waters of the Atlantic all the way to the Antarctic. Having enjoyed some of the best weather and sailing conditions of the whole voyage, Ben is enjoying the company of his new crewmates and life aboard *Northabout* is as near perfect as ocean sailing gets, as evidenced in the many blogs now appearing, littered with praise for the scenery, the wildlife and the exceptional quality of the food on board. On 27 September Ben writes:

Today was a perfect, and I mean perfect, day. I was woken up at half three in the morning in time for my watch which, while cold, was clear with a decent view of the northern lights and a clear, bright crescent moon. My downtime in-between involved jumping whales, a beautiful sunrise, warm day and the invention of the tuna-mayo-chutney sandwich. Just after dinner I went up into the cockpit and noticed that we had the best aurora I've ever seen. It was astonishing. We all got up into the cockpit and saw the most epic display of charged particles colliding with the ionosphere that anyone could possibly hope to see. It was the best day of the expedition. By far.

But as with so many things at sea, at the start of the voyage home, the weather gods had even yet a surprise or two up their sleeves. After almost a week of perfect sailing weather the charts show a massive low building in the North Atlantic directly in their intended path.

ROB HUDSON'S BLOG
4 October 2016

We left the weather station early yesterday morning in grey, wet, miserable conditions – a stark contrast to the glorious weather of the last 10 days. Maybe Greenland was trying to tell us something. My first watch was from 1400 to 1600, and was quite an experience. I attached my harness before leaving the main cabin and attached the second hook to another point near the wheel, and then took over from David. Looking around at the conditions a loud "Yeehaaar!" left my mouth and was whipped away by the wind. The seas were magnificent, lashed by the wind and spewing spume from the top, as Northabout gamely reached across the tops under reefed staysail. I vowed before this trip to savour every second to the full, and that was two hours I will remember for ever, believe it or not in a good way. The whole adventure has been amazing, but this is what it is really about.

GREENLAND   ICELAND

approximate position
of Northabout

Computer generated image of the Atlantic storm on 4 October.

In fact the storm continues throughout the period from the 4–6 October with gusts reaching over 50 knots and a 7 metre sea – with relatively quiet periods between. Mike Stewart recorded his thoughts in the ship's log:

We have handled this at 50 KT with around 7m seas, (occasionally 8-9m) so our confidence levels are good. I heaved the boat to for a few minutes to test how she behaved, and she was 'OK' sitting duck like as the rollers powered through beneath us. During the evening, we were hit by one breaker, as always, there's a set bigger than the rest, and of course one broke over the boat, we were lifted and pushed sideways like a cork, but did not go over to any degree, which says volumes for our stability curve. The longer range predictions are good for our run to Ireland. We could have waited in Greenland, but as we only do 6 knots, and our ETA is in around 7 days, sooner or later we would have had to deal with rough weather, it has now been done while we are fresh, and well fed, and alert. Well done to Northabout, a tough old girl, and Crew, especially 'Youngest' Ben, who deserves a skipper's 'mention in dispatches', at least, for 'steadiness under pressure on watch' and remaining on deck when required. He also went forward in big seas, to fix an issue with the main halyard without question, was safe the whole time and sorted out the job smartly and professionally as I expected of this talented lad. Well done Ben!.

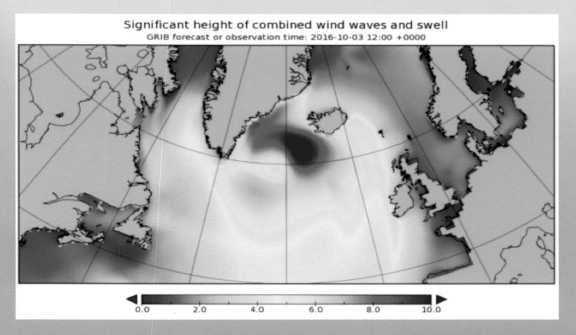

Satellite image of the Atlantic storm on 4 October and (right) imagery of the sea conditions at the start of the crossing.

WHUMP! A WALL OF WATER KNOCKS US
SIDEWAYS AND WATER IS EVERYWHERE
LIKE SOMEONE HAS A FIRE HOSE
SPRAYING ON US...

The crew in survival suits, Ben makes light of the situation during the Kara Sea hurricane.

Asked some months later about his own most scary moments during the whole of the PoC voyage, Ben is remarkably self-possessed:

Rather disappointingly for those looking for dramatic effect I wasn't scared at any point in the trip, including at the height of the storms – both the hurricane in the Kara Sea and during the Atlantic storm. The photo of Constance, Ros, Barbara and myself in our survival suits, with myself playing around, is pretty much a reflection of how I felt – though there was a point when I was sure we were all going to die. The first 48 hours of the Atlantic crossing, when for days we had water rushing past the port holes in the saloon, I don't think anyone on board was particularly worried. The important thing is to ensure you know what to do when these situations arise and to put into practice the advice and drills that any competent sailor will have learned.

Then, as the storm cleared to the north – and as had happened at the end of the North East Passage – a steady headwind hampered forward progress just when the end of the trip seemed in sight. From 5–10 October these winds persisted, resulting in Mike talking down all sails and resorting to the engine, its constant vibration adding to the frustration of those on board. In all, the winds had taken *Northabout* on a more northwesterly course than had been planned and now, as they sailed south under power, after four months, most of the time at sea, Ben was looking out eagerly for sign of landfall:

At this rate the chart plotter estimates it'll take us just over five days to get to Ireland. Combining the experience of the last few months and the three days of my first ocean passage I've come to the conclusion that while for many of us sailing for short periods

BEN'S BLOG
15 October 2016

So we're in Ireland! We arrived in the charmingly named Blacksod harbour. There to meet us were some of the men who built and sailed Northabout *round the North Pole the first time, Jarlath Cunnane, Michael Brogan and Tom Moran. They'd all come round from their respective homes in Westport to say hi and bring us food. We all then went to a nearby pub. The following hours convinced me that I should have visited Ireland long ago. They're all so friendly!*

of time, a day, a week, a month and so on, is enjoyable, in order to want, and continue to want, sailing as a profession requires someone with a very unusual frame of mind, and while I do enjoy sailing I am not of that ilk. So to any professional crew out there I must say that while I am very impressed by you all, that when I get home I'm going to run and hide somewhere where the ground is stable for a good few weeks.

And then, as David Hempleman-Adams later put it: 'Almost as though drawn by some mystic Celtic compass, *Northabout* heads not for her intended landfall in Ireland but, by dint of all those headwinds, fetches up a stone's throw from her home port, the very place where Jarlath Cunnane first laid her keel.'

Above: A convivial evening with Jaralath and crew in Blacksod. Left: Northabout *entering Blacksod harbour.*

Sea Dogs. Ben and Jarlath Cunnane aboard the vessel he'd built, sailing for Westport.

147

The spectacular Dingle coastline.

Rob, Steve, Ben and David at the South Pole Inn which was once owned by Tom Crean, one of Captain Scott's and Ernest Shakleton's colleagues on their expeditions to the Antarctic. The inn is full of memorabilia and photographs from the period.

And it wasn't long before for Jarlath and his the Irish crew turned up to greet their old vessel taking the new arrivals to a local hostelry for a few pints and a traditional Irish sing-song. Ben was delighted to see Frances Gard turn up out of the blue, among the first to congratulate him on the completion of his journey.

With Steve Edwards joining the crew for the trip home to Bristol, they first stop to sample the delights of Irish hospitality both in Blacksod, then Westport (including a trip to the South Pole Inn at Annascaul), and finally to Dingle. Then, on 17 October after 20 weeks at sea and covering 13 500 miles, *Northabout* is set on her course for Portishead and Bristol:

The next morning we set off with high spirits. We'd had a look at the weather forecast and it was tailwinds all the way, for once. The next twenty four hours moved us very very quickly towards our target, Dad got seasick but fortunately that didn't last long. With the wind and swell behind us we were doing twelve knots at times with an average of about seven. Amazingly that continued and continues to continue as we continue to head east. We're now in the lee of Wales and hope to get to Portishead tomorrow. Thence to Bristol, see you there!

The Atlantic crew celebrate their arrival in Portishead.

*　　　*　　　*

A crew reunion and smiles all round for the press. Many of the former PoC crew members turned up including David Hempleman-Adams and an offical 'welcome home' was given by the city's mayor.

Homecoming.

As *Northabout* made her way back under Brunel's suspension bridge there were people coming out to see her home, waving from the quays alongside the Severn. And as she tied up in the shadow of the SS *Great Britain*, here were echoes of a great maritime history; of daring feats and significant challenges overcome. For Ben, arriving back to be greeted by his fellow crewmates with whom he shared various legs of the voyage and a melee of eager press he had little time to reflect on his personal achievement. Sure, it spelt the end of an unforgettable journey – but for him simply a stepping stone to further adventures.

What Next?

Personal Reflections on My Voyage & on Journeys Ahead

"Twenty years from now you will be more disappointed by the things you didn't do than by the ones you did do. So throw off the bowlines. Sail away from the safe harbor. Catch the trade winds in your sails. Explore. Dream. Discover."

...attributed to Mark Twain

IN THE MONTHS SINCE MY RETURN from the Polar Ocean Challenge I've had time to reflect on my journey, both on what it meant to me at the time and also on how it has changed me, my outlook on life, and my attitude towards others.

I suppose one might like to imagine that being thrown in at the deep end – almost literally as far as some parts of the voyage were concerned – would have an immediate and profound effect on one, something almost tangible which I recognised within myself and that one's friends and family instantly remarked upon. Not true.

The fact is that I returned to the prospect of a busy year at school, with GCSEs looming meaning that I had to put thoughts of the voyage on the back burner. Nor did my friends at school seem all that interested in what I'd been up to – even those who

A complete change of gear – trying out a friend's Ducati.

Our beautiful family home in the Lake District provided a haven where, after returning from the voyage, I was able to spend some quiet time reflecting on what the voyage had meant and what the future might hold. Here my oldest brother and I take a walk amid Cumbria's superb scenery.

had been aware of my part in the Polar Ocean Challenge knew only that I'd spent my summer on a boat, possibly somewhere cold, and having something to do with a 'pole'. It's only with the passage of time that I've come to appreciate that the voyage was indeed one of self-discovery. As the man said "Travel far enough and you end up meeting yourself" – and that's certainly been true for me.

Almost immediately after tying up in Bristol preparing for exams was pretty much all consuming, up to the point, as I write this, I've had little else to occupy my thoughts. I wouldn't describe myself as a natural academic but I do have the capacity to learn and certainly an aspiration to follow a passion for what used be called the 'natural sciences', now divided into the various branches of physics, chemistry, biology and earth sciences. It is the first of these that I find most attractive – a chance to achieve a greater understanding of how the world works – an interest I hope to follow academically although perhaps not as a career. I simply relish the idea of pursuing a subject for its own sake, particularly if one is being taught by people who are at the top of their game.

While my schoolfriends, much to my relief and in part due to their own exam preparations, show a healthy disregard for my polar exploits, my family had other reasons for not dwelling on my role in them. For a start, my mother Ros, and father Steve had their own reflecting to do on the voyage having taken part in various legs and each having their own views as to what it meant to them. Besides contemplating the rigours and delights of the trip itself they, unlike me, had spent months both before and during the voyage attending to the refitting of the vessel and equipping her. No doubt they had thoughts for my safety in the back of their minds and, knowing them as I do, they left nothing to chance and prepared everything meticulously. They also had my impending demands of schoolwork in mind.

Playing with fire 1. For a time I had contemplated, for the summer holidays, joining a troupe of travelling entertainers skilled in acrobatics, fire-eating and so on. Here I entertain a crowd at the 'Buttermere Bash' Paragliding Festival with a fire-stick demonstration.

Playing with fire 2. Barbecuing for the family while in the Lakes. Anyone seen my light-sabre?

But, as time passes, I realise more and more just how much the PoC had changed me and appreciate that to be privileged enough to have the opportunity to undertake such an adventure and not submit to self-reflection would pose the obvious question: Why do it?

I see that one of the greatest changes in me has been my willingness to put up with discomfort. Being comfortable seems far less important to me now that it did before and overall I'd say I'm much happier putting up with other peoples' idiosyncracies than I was prior to the trip. I'm sure that this comes from being aboard *Northabout* working alongside a wide mix of individuals living in a confined space, where functioning as a team was critical to the venture's success. Observing the differences in behaviour between my crewmates, particularly in times of stress, and being able to react oneself tolerantly and rationally is a life-lesson well worth learning. And of course, recognising that others are having to make the same allowances for you is not an easy thing to accept, especially for a fourteen year old.

Back among friends taking a midnight dip in the lake. The voyage on board Northabout *made me appreciate the importance of family ties, and the value of close friendships. Accepting the faults in others while recognising your own shortcomings is a vital life-lesson.*

The downside to this is having to remember, when you're back among your contemporaries, that it's normal for teenagers to be annoyed by minor discomforts and consumed by trivialities – so you do sometimes feel somewhat 'apart'. This means having to bury that side of my life that might otherwise create a sense of separation from friends. Patronising? I hope not – but this is definitely a consequence of having such a profound experience at such a young age.

Listening to and learning from others is part of growing – but chosing WHO to learn from is even more important. The weeks aboard Northabout *provided plenty of opportunity to observe my crewmates and to take note of how the tough times brought the best out of the best. Some people you would have no hesitation in sailing with again. Here I am back in Greenland in the summer of 2017 with David Hempleman-Adams and my mother, Ros, aboard the RIB. On this trip we called in at Qaanaag and Siorapaluk (Greenland's most northerly settlement).*

*　　*　　*

From a purely practical point of view the voyage gave me both the skill and confidence to handle a sailing boat in just about any conditions, from weaving through ice to helming in a major storm, something that no sailing courses could ever provide. While there were one or two occasions when we might all have died my thoughts, even at the most critical moments, were pretty much along the lines "If I survive this, it will be a great experience!"

Ben at home with his brothers and sisters.

Ben with Maureen Small on the dockside in Lerwick, Shetland Islands, in 2017. Maureen, an old schoolfriend of David Hempleman-Adams, now lives in Lerwick and works in Whiteness School. It was Maureen who arranged Ben's promised return visit to the school a year after Northabout *and her crew had stopped off in Lerwick on the first leg of the Polar Ocean Challenge.*

I also gained insight into leadership skills, observing the different ways in which David Hempleman-Adams, Nikolai and our other skippers worked with the crew to get the most out of each individually while also maintaining the best teamwork. I learnt that while one can always find a competent sailor to get you across the Atlantic, finding four competent sailors to do so without tearing each others' throats out is quite a different skill. And so I guess the lesson is, select the best people you can but expect the worst to happen.

* * *

Apart from the welcome opportunity to promote the aims of the Polar Ocean Challenge and Wicked Weather Watch I really enjoy telling others about my voyage and find that presenting comes easily to me. But I admit, getting a standing ovation from my fellow students at my own school at the end of one presentation did come as a bit of a surprise.

These photos show my return to Whiteness School in Lerwick where I had given my original talk to the students on the first leg of the PoC. This time I was able to describe to them the whole of my adventure and also joined them for lunch.

157

Looking back but moving forward – return to Greenland aboard Northabout *2017.*

What next? Well, I'm still involved both with Wicked Weather Watch and the Addenbrooke's Charitable Trust, giving illustrated talks about my adventure whenever invited, particularly enjoying school visits for this purpose. I will shortly be returning to the school in Lerwick which I visited on our first leg of the Polar Ocean Challenge.

Immediately we have plans as a family to make a crossing of the Greenland ice cap. It will be a delight to make a return to the world's largest island, not only for its stupendous scenery but for the fascinating lives of its people and their history, not least the legends associated with the place.

And with this in mind, I'm also looking forward to working with a new charity being set up by, among others, David Hempleman-Adams and my mother, Ros, which is to be named Kiviuq, after one of Greenland's mythological heroes. This new charity will provide young people, regardless of background and financial situation, an opportunity to share in adventures similar to that I have experienced by taking them on sailing courses. Here they will learn not only to handle sailing boats but also survival skills, leading to the gaining of First Aid and Competent Crew certificates. Eventually there will be a more ambitious course held in Greenland aboard *Northabout* – bringing a nice symmetry to this new venture from a personal perspective.

*   *   *

I know I've been fortunate in being given the opportunity to sail aboard *Northabout* on her epic voyage. I hope readers of this book will also find it in themselves to 'throw off the bowlines and seek to explore, dream, discover'.

Acknowledgements

LOOKING AT THIS BOOK NOW, just before it goes for printing, I am struck by a strong sense of gratitude to all the people who allowed me to be part of an extraordinary expedition, went through it with me in both thick and thin, and then those that helped so much with creating the book. They are, of course, too many to name so I can only apologise if you have been left out and hope you will understand.

First very many thanks to Simon Butler for listening, organising my memories, setting them out and integrating them so well with the vast number of pictures from the expedition, I am overjoyed with the result. To my publisher Steven Pugsley for all your support with the book, it wouldn't have happened without the two of you.

Thanks to Nikolai Litau and Mike Stewart who skippered the boat and kept us all safe in the worst times, to the many crew who put up with me and supported me through the long journey, Francis Gard for all the work on our media efforts, organising the records etc. and to the team that prepared the boat. A special mention is due to my school (St Chris in Letchworth) for having the vision to allow me to go and doing the work to help me with the academic consequences. Thanks also to Jarleth, Tom and Michael, the original Irish builders and crew of such a tough boat as *Northabout*, and for their extraordinary welcome when I most needed it.

I would like to thank my parents for being brave enough (or negligent enough) to allow me to go on the expedition and for their support through the whole project. As lots of very sensible adults have told me, there are not that many parents who would have done this.

And lastly I must thank David Hempleman-Adams, without whom none of this would have happened. It is David's vision and drive that created the Polar Ocean Challenge expedition and his kindness and trust that gave me the chance to be part of it. I am profoundly grateful.

Ben Edwards
2018